D0122701

The Urban American Indian

The Urban
American Indian

Alan L. Sorkin
The Johns Hopkins University
and the University of Maryland
Baltimore County

Lexington Books
D.C. Heath and Company
Lexington, Massachusetts
Toronto

Library of Congress Cataloging in Publication Data

Sorkin, Alan L.
   The urban American Indian.

   Includes index.
   1. Indians of North America—Urban residence. I. Title.
E98.U72S67   301.45'19'7073   76-54459
ISBN 0-669-01296-3

Published simultaneously in Canada.

Printed in the United States of America.

International Standard Book Number: 0-669-01296-3

Library of Congress Catalog Card Number: 76-54459

Contents

List of Tables

Preface

Most of the recent literature dealing with the economic and social problems of American Indians focuses on those native Americans residing on reservations. In contrast, this book is concerned with the other 50 percent of the American Indian population—those who live in urban areas.

Chapter 1 provides an historical introduction to the study. The principal events and legislation affecting Indians are presented in historical context. The second chapter compares the economic and social progress of urban as opposed to reservation Indians. It is found that such variables as income, occupational status, and educational attainment indicate greater improvement for urban as opposed to reservation Indians. Chapter 3 focuses on manpower and relocation programs operated by the government to encourage movement from the reservations to urban areas. These programs are evaluated using a variety of criteria. Chapter 4 is concerned with the problems of urban Indian health and alcoholism. Although data are limited, there is some evidence that Indian health is worse in urban areas in comparison to reservations. The fifth chapter considers housing and social services available to urban Indians. In both these areas severe problems exist with very limited resources available to improve the situation. Chapter 6 discusses urban Indian education. In spite of the considerable federal expenditure in this area there has been very little evaluation of the effectiveness of this investment. Chapter 7 focuses on the development of urban Indian institutions. Particular attention is given to the growth of Indian centers and their role in native community development. The eighth chapter discusses the problems of acculturation and adjustment of urban Indians. Several case studies are presented. The final chapter summarizes earlier findings and provides suggestions for future research. In addition, some suggested changes in federal policy regarding urban Indians are presented.

The author is grateful to the following authors and journals for permission to quote copyrighted material: Tony Lazewski, The Association of American Geographers, *Human Organization, Minnesota Medicine*, and *The Indian Historian.*

Mike McCarroll and Martin Sorkin read the entire manuscript. Their constructive comments are greatly appreciated, but the author is solely responsible for any errors. Peggy Bremer and Josephine Drecchio typed the several drafts of the manuscript in an excellent manner. The manuscript was edited by Sheila Marian, and the index was prepared by Jack Gates.

1 Historical Introducton

Most urban Indians were born or raised on reservations and subsequently moved to the city. The policies and programs of the federal government in regard to the reservations clearly have a direct impact on the quality of life of the Indians living there. Moreover, these policies also affect the attitudes of urban migrants in regard to the usefulness of social programs and their general feelings toward the dominant (non-Indian culture). Thus it is useful to briefly examine in historical context the major aspects of federal Indian policy.

The desire for Indian land and other resources has been the most important reason for most of the early disputes between Indians and whites and federal and state governments. Pressured by President Andrew Jackson, Congress passed the Indian Removal Act of 1830 in the belief that separation of the races would limit conflict and that land would be available for white settlement in the east.[1] The Indian lands, which reached a peak of 150 million acres in 1873, are known as reservations.[2]

Reservations are tribally owned lands, ranging from less than one acre (Strawberry Valley Rancheria in California) to about 25,000 square miles (the Navajo Reservation, with an estimated 120,000 Indians occupying an area embracing parts of Arizona, New Mexico and Utah—a tract about the size of West Virginia). There are approximately 160 reservations. Most of them were established before 1871 by treaties between the United States and the Indians as the non-Indian moved west in his search for more land; others were founded later by federal statutes, presidential orders, or agreements approved by Congress. Indians living on reservations have nearly all the freedoms other Americans possess; restrictions are placed only on tribal funds and property.

Secretary of War Henry Knox was given responsibility for Indian affairs in 1789, but territorial governors retained some authority over Indian agents. The office of superintendent of Indian trade was established in 1806 and abolished in 1822. Two years later, Secretary of War John C. Calhoun ordered the creation of the Bureau of Indian Affairs (BIA). Congress created the position of Commissioner of Indian Affairs in 1832 and a Department of Indian Affairs in 1834, both of which were to be transferred to the Department of the Interior upon its establishment in 1849.[3] The commissioner has been a presidential appointee responsible to the secretary of the interior.[a]

The Bureau of Indian Affairs provides many of the services that non-Indians

---

[a]In 1977 the title of Commissioner of Indian Affairs was abolished and the person with that responsibility was given the title Assistant Secretary of Interior for Indian Affairs.

1

receive from state and local government. Each of its functions, such as social services, education, and industrial development is the responsibility of a separate division. Reservation programs are administered by ten area directors.

From 1880 until 1934 the federal government put strong pressure on Indian tribes to discard their traditional customs and to be assimilated into American society. The General Allotment Act of 1887 (the Dawes Act) which remained the instrument of federal Indian policy for thirty years, permitted the breaking up of tribal or reservation land into individual allotments if the president believed the land could thereby be advantageously employed. Each head of a family was eligible for 80 acres of agricultural land or 160 acres of grazing land.[4]

The deed to the land was retained by the federal government for twenty-five years, or longer if the president thought an extension necessary. At the end of this period the title to the land was given to the Indian along with his citizenship. Lands not allotted to individual Indians were declared surplus and opened up to homesteading. It was believed that pressuring Indians to become individual farm operators would accelerate their assimilation into the dominant culture and help to make them productive members of the community.

Because many Indians had little interest in agriculture and their farms were too small to yield an adequate income, numerous allotments were sold at low prices. By 1933, 91 million acres, two-thirds of the Indian land base, had passed into non-Indian hands.[5]

At this time education of Indian children took place in off-reservation boarding schools. This was considered another method in which assimilation was to be accomplished. "This educational model for Indian youth was directed at developing young men and women who could join the mainstream of non-Indian society. Instead it left a legacy of frustration, depression and alienation that made Indians unable to pursue the traditions of their fathers, but left them unequipped to participate in white dominated society."[6]

In 1934 the Dawes Act was repealed and replaced by the Indian Reorganization Act (the Wheeler-Howard Act). This law reflecting the belief that "the tribal Indian remains the self-reliant and self-supporting Indian," provided for strengthening tribal governments and stated new economic policies. The trust period on Indian land was continued indefinitely, and those lands remaining unsold after allotment were returned to the tribes. The act authorized the establishment of a revolving loan fund to provide credit for agricultural and industrial enterprises.

Also during the 1930s the education of children in their home environment became more common as many small day schools were built on the reservations.

Many Indian lands are still held in trust by the federal government. The erroneous belief thus persists that Indians are wards of the federal government. Since 1924 all Indians have been citizens of the United States and have the right to vote in state and federal elections, as well as the responsibility to serve in the Armed Forces. Indians must pay the same taxes as non-Indians except that trust property and income derived from it are exempt from taxation.

After World War II, Indian perceptions of reservations and cities began to change. The war showed many Indians a world quite different from the typical isolated reservation. There were opportunities for achievement in the military service and defense industries that had never existed on the reservations. Given the limited development of the reservations many Indians left to work in the cities. For example, by 1951, more than seventeen thousand Navajos worked away from the reservation.[7]

During the early and mid 1950s, there was considerable pressure for terminating federal responsibility for Indian reservations, and programs for reservation development were temporarily suspended. After the disastrous results of forced termination of two important tribes (the Klamaths and Menominees) became known, federal termination efforts waned and reservation development programs were reinstituted.[8]

During this period the federal government believed that the level of reservation resources were inadequate to support the existing population.[9] Thus a large scale relocation program was instituted in 1952 to remove the "surplus" labor and expand economic opportunity. The program still operates today. It provides employment and training in major metropolitan areas where job opportunities have tended to be abundant.

Federal agencies (principally the Bureau of Indian Affairs) spend over $1 billion annually to provide services to reservation Indians. In general, existing programs give Indians more freedom to decide where they will raise their families (on or off reservations) than did any programs in earlier years. The federal government does not, in balance, either encourage or discourage Indians from leaving the reservations. Expectations and desires for self-fulfillment vary so greatly among tribes and among their members that programs have been devised to give the individual Indian a choice about where he earns his livelihood.

The Merian report nearly fifty years ago took the position that "the work with and for the Indians must give consideration to the desires of the individual Indians. He who wishes to merge into the social and economic life of the prevailing civilization of this country should be given all practicable aid and advice in making the necessary adjustments. He who wants to remain an Indian and live according to his old culture should be aided in doing so."[10]

The recent history of federal and state governmental relations with reservation Indians shows a progressive elimination of restrictions. In 1938 seven states refused to let Indians vote; however, by 1948 all seven had removed their restrictions. The Indian Claims Commission Act of 1946 finally permitted tribes to sue the federal government. Unfair dealings in lands have been the major charge in such suits. Another restriction on reservation Indians, imposed in 1802, authorized the president to regulate the selling of alcoholic beverages among the tribes. That authority, broadened and strengthened over the years, ultimately (by Act of July 23, 1892, as amended in 1938) prohibited the sale or gift of liquor to Indians. The validity of the Indian liquor law was upheld by the

Supreme Court on several occasions by a broad interpretation of Congress' power to regulate commerce with Indian tribes. However, by 1953, Indians were treated just the same as non-Indians when off the reservation (except where state laws singled them out) and were granted the right of local option for their reservations.[11]

One major restriction on reservation Indians remains. Congress has imposed limitations on their disposal of trust or restricted property. Administrative or Congressional approval is required for the sale of such property or the expenditure of certain trust funds. Unless this restriction is eliminated (with appropriate safeguards), the Indians will continue to be denied full citizenship rights and will remain in a sense a dependent people.

The most important research project ever undertaken in regard to Indian affairs was completed in 1928 by the Institute for Government Research. The study, known as the Meriam Report, documented the dismal socioeconomic status of reservation Indians and the failures of federal Indian policy. This report resulted in a substantial increase in appropriations for programs operated by the Bureau of Indian Affairs. The study also gave impetus to the passage of the Indian Reorganization Act.

While the Meriam Report accurately reflected the conditions of life on the reservations, the findings on the status of migrated (urban Indians) give the impression of rapid assimilation and living standards nearly as high as the whites.[12] With regard to the latter conclusion, Meriam and his associates were probably wrong. A hearing held in 1928 at Riverside, California by the Senate Subcommittee of the Committee on Indian Affairs indicates the unsatisfactory conditions for urban Indians.[13] Such problems as poor housing, employment discrimination, and lack of social services for nonreservation Indians were frequently mentioned. In retrospect it is regrettable that the federal government chose to base much of its off-reservation policy on the Meriam Report rather than on the hearings. The former concluded that "no effort should be directed toward building up an independent organization for aiding migrating Indians but rather toward establishing cooperative relations with existing agencies which serve the population as a whole."[14] The subsequent migration of Indians to the cities was to be a more painful experience as a direct result of the thinking underlying this recommendation.

Before the passage of the Snyder Act of 1921 there had been no specific authorization for the appropriation and expenditure for most of the programs that the Bureau of Indian Affairs had come to maintain for the benefit of Indians. In the Congress appropriations for the Bureau of Indian Affairs were subject to a point-by-point congressional review that was time consuming and inefficient. This frustrating process was partly improved by passage of the Snyder Act which authorized items of appropriations in nine broad program areas:

The Bureau of Indian Affairs, under the supervision of the Secretary of the Interior, shall direct, supervise, and expend such monies as Congress may from time to time appropriate, for the benefit, care, and assistance of the Indians throughout the United States for the following purposes:

General support and civilization, including education.

For relief of distress and conservation of health.

For industrial assistance and advancement and general administration of Indian property.

For extension, improvement, operation and maintenance of existing Indian irrigation systems and for development of water supplies.

For the enlargement, extension, improvement, and repair of the buildings and grounds of existing plants and projects.

For the employment of inspectors, supervisors, superintendents, clerks, field matrons, farmers, physicians, Indian police, Indian judges, and other employees.

For the suppression of traffic in intoxicating liquor and deleterious drugs.

For the purchase of horse-drawn and motor-propelled passenger carrying vehicles for official use.

And for general and incidental expenses in connection with the administration of Indian affairs.[15]

A relevant interpretation of the act was made in December 1971 by the assistant solicitor of the Department of the Interior, Mr. Charles Soller. In a written opinion to the commissioner of Indian Affairs, Mr. Soller stated that:

On its face, the underscored language is abundantly clear and requires no interpretation. Literally it authorizes the expenditure of funds for purposes within the named program categories for the benefit of any and all Indians, of whatever degree, whether or not members of federally recognized tribes, and without regard to residence so long as they are within the United States. . . . With language so unequivocal, it is subject to the general rule of the law that plain and unambiguous language will be followed.[16]

The opinion indicates that the Snyder Act makes urban Indians eligible for Bureau of Indian Affairs services but it cautions the bureau against extending BIA services to all Indians without first considering other "statutory limitations" and without first consulting with appropriate congressional committees. Apparently, however, the bureau never got a chance to take those other two steps because the commissioner received direct instruction from then assistant secretary of the interior, Harrison Loesch, not to divert the bureau's "attention and limited funds from our basic responsibility" of serving only on-reservation

Indians. However, as explained in considerable detail by the Supreme Court in *Morton* v. *Ruiz*, the provision of BIA services "clearly has not been limited to reservation Indians" only. In fact, native Americans in Oklahoma and Alaska have always received BIA services and participated in the Public Health Service's comprehensive health program for Indians, whether they live on or off the reservation.

It is true that the court in the *Ruiz* case did not interpret the Snyder Act as requiring the bureau to provide its social service program benefits to all Indians. However, it is equally true that the decision interpreted the Snyder Act in sufficiently broad terms that such an application would be entirely permissible. It stated that: "We need not approach the issue in terms of whether Congress intended for all Indians, regardless of residence and the degree of assimilation, to be covered by the general assistance program. We need only ascertain the intent of Congress with respect to those Indian claimants in the case before us."[17]

Thus, the Supreme Court chose to avoid a definitive judgment on the overall issue by merely indicating that the Bureau of Indian Affairs has the duty to provide general assistance services to Indians living "on or near the reservation" and who maintain close economic and social ties to the reservation and are assimilated.

The argument in favor of providing special programs of assistance to urban Indians has two facets. The case can be made on the basis of special needs and on the basis of unique Indian rights. The argument that considers Indian rights in off-reservation settings is very controversial and it will undoubtedly require a number of court decisions or legislation before the question is finally decided. However, the issue of needs is immediate and undeniable. Regardless of how the legal argument is resolved, the government is still confronted by the problem of recognizing that the relocation program and the impoverished reservations have resulted in the emergence of some 500,000 nonreservation Indians whose needs are in most cases not being met by existing agencies. It must decide the best way in which a program can be established and operated to ensure that these needs are not ignored.

Notes

1. Act of May 28, 1830, 4 Stat. 411.
2. Oliver La Farge, *As Long as the Grass Shall Grow* (New York: Alliance Book Co., 1940), p. 30.
3. Lawrence F. Schmeckebier, *The Office of Indian Affairs: Its History, Activities and Organization* (Baltimore: The Johns Hopkins Press, 1927), pp. 26-28 and 43.
4. Theodore H. Haas, "The Legal Aspects of Indian Affairs from 1887 to 1957," in George E. Simpson and J. Milton Yinger, eds., *American Indians and*

American Life, Annals of the American Academy of Political and Social Science 311 (May 1975):13.

5. Ibid.

6. Indian Education Task Force Five, *Final Report to the American Indian Policy Review Commission on Indian Education* (Washington, D.C.: U.S. Government Printing Office, 1976), p. 431.

7. Ibid., pp. 431-432.

8. William A. Brophy and Sophy D. Aberle, comps., *The Indian: America's Unfinished Business* (Ardmore: University of Oklahoma Press, 1966), pp. 196, 201-202, and 206-207.

9. U.S. Congress, House Committee on Interior and Insular Affairs, *Survey Report on the Bureau of Indian Affairs* (Washington, D.C.: U.S. Government Printing Office, 1954), p. 23.

10. Institute for Government Research, *The Problem of Indian Administration* (Baltimore: The Johns Hopkins Press, 1928), p. 88.

11. Haas, "Legal Aspects of Indian Affairs," pp. 16-17.

12. Institute for Government Research, *Problem of Indian Administration*, chapter 12.

13. Urban and Rural Non-Reservation Indians Task Force Eight, *Final Report to the American Indian Policy Review Commission on Urban and Rural Non-Reservation Indians* (Washington, D.C.: U.S. Government Printing Office, 1976), p. 9.

14. Institute for Government Research, *Problem of Indian Administration*, p. 669.

15. Urban and Rural Non-Reservation Indians Task Force Eight, *Final Report on Urban and Rural Non-Reservation Indians*, p. 9.

16. Ibid.

17. Ibid., p. 10.

2

The Economic and Social Status of the Urban American Indian

The native American population of North America at the time of Columbus is generally estimated to have been approximately 850,000.[1] However, by 1890, this figure had declined to about 240,000, reflecting the effects of war, disease and poverty. Since that time, the Indian population has increased with the gain becoming very rapid in recent years (see table 2-1).

Some of the fluctuations in the above population statistics are primarily the result of differing census procedures used to classify persons as Indians. For example, in 1960 and 1970 information was obtained primarily through self-enumeration. Respondents classified themselves with respect to race, and nonrespondents were interviewed by telephone or direct visit. For persons of mixed parentage who were in doubt as to their racial classification, the race of the person's father was used. Prior to 1960, racial identification was made on the basis of observation by enumerators who may not have appropriately identified Indians living off reservations.[2]

On the basis of the ratio of children to women in the Indian population, it is unlikely that the average annual birth rate is above thirty-five per thousand. Allowance for mortality would suggest that not more than three-fourths of the indicated 1960-1970 population gain resulted from natural increase. Some of the remaining increase could reflect immigration, but most of the remainder is unexplained.[3]

The Meriam Report observed that small numbers of Indians were living in cities in 1926, most of them close to reservations (Winslow, Arizona; Gallup, New Mexico; Needles, California; Phoenix, Arizona; Albuquerque, New Mexico; and Santa Fe, New Mexico), and only a few in the large cities some distance from reservations, such as Los Angeles, California; Minneapolis, Minnesota; and Milwaukee, Wisconsin. It was estimated that less than ten thousand Indians lived in urban communities.[4]

Except for the 1930-1940 decade (when severe urban unemployment may have forced some urban Indians to return to the reservation), the percentage of Indians living in cities has steadily increased. If current trends continue, the proportion of Indians living in urban areas will likely exceed 50 percent by 1980. Part of the rapid increase in the number of Indians residing in cities since 1950 is due to a federally assisted relocation program operated by the Bureau of Indian Affairs. However, many Indians have moved from the reservations to urban locations without any public assistance.

During the 1960-1970 decade an especially rapid growth in the Indian

9

Table 2-1
Indian Population of the United States, 1890-1977
(in thousands)

Year	Total	Urban	Rural	Percent Urban
1890	248	–	–	–
1900	237	1	236	0.4
1910	266	12	254	4.5
1920	244	15	229	6.1
1930	332	33	299	9.9
1940	334	24	310	7.2
1950	343	56	287	13.4
1960	524	146	378	27.9
1970	764	340	424	44.5
1977[a]	1,000	500	500	50.0

Sources: Elain Neils, "The Urbanization of the American Indian and the Federal Program of Relocation Assistance" (Master's thesis, University of Chicago, 1969), p.23; U.S. Department of Commerce, Bureau of the Census, 1970 Census of Population, *American Indians* (Washington, D.C.: U.S. Government Printing Office, 1973), table 1, p. 1.
[a]Estimated.

population occurred in various cities (see table 2-2). This population increase has continued during the 1970s.

Indian organizations and various native American spokesmen question the census figures and claim that they understate the urban Indian population by a considerable margin. It is indicated that many urban Indians do not complete the census forms and are not available for interviews because they have no fixed address in the city or simply don't want to be interviewed. In addition, the large transient population that moves from the city to the reservation and back again makes accurate population figures difficult to obtain.

The most rapid percentage increase in urban Indian population has occurred in cities located on the West Coast. Although part of the increase in Los Angeles-Long Beach and San Francisco-Oakland results from the fact that these cities are places where the BIA relocates Indians for purposes of training and employment, this phenomenon does not account for all of the population gain. Thus, cities like San Diego, California and Seattle, Washington have experienced rapid gains in the number of Indians, but neither of these cities participated in the BIA relocation program. It is likely that climate and rapidly expanding labor markets have accounted for a large part of the movement of Indians to the West Coast.

Los Angeles attracts Indians from all over the United States. Thus, Price found Indians there from over one hundred tribes with the largest number from

Table 2-2
Indian Population, Selected Cities, 1960, 1970, and 1976

City	1960 Population	1970 Population	Percentage Increase 1960-1970	1976[a] Population
Oklahoma City	4,355	12,951	197	–
Los Angeles-Long Beach	4,130	23,908	479	40,000-75,000
Chicago	3,394	8,203	141	20,000
Minneapolis	2,007	9,911	377	14,000
Buffalo	1,931	5,606	190	–
Albuquerque	1,848	5,822	215	18,000
Seattle	1,729	8,814	409	17,000
San Francisco-Oakland	2,234	12,041	439	45,000-55,000
Dallas	1,466	5,500	275	10,000-12,000
New York	3,262	9,984	261	–
San Diego	1,083	6,007	454	–
Denver	1,133	4,104	278	10,000

Sources: Elaine Neils, "The Urbanization of the American Indian and the Federal Program of Relocation Assistance" (Master's thesis, University of Chicago, 1969), pp. 184-185; and U.S. Department of Commerce, Bureau of the Census, 1970 Census of Population, *American Indians* (Washington, D.C.: U.S. Government Printing Office, 1973), table 1, p. 1 and table 11, pp. 138-140.

[a]Estimated by various urban organizations. See Urban and Rural Non-Reservation Indians Task Force Eight, *Final Report to the American Indian Policy Review Commission on Urban and Rural Non-Reservation Indians* (Washington, D.C.: U.S. Government Printing Office, 1976), pp. 106-133.

the Navajo, Sioux, and five civilized tribes (Cherokee, Choctaw, Chickasaw, Creek, and Seminole). There were a large number of plains Indians (for example, Sioux) as well as members of such eastern groups as the Nanticokes.[5]

The present Indian population of the Los Angeles area consists primarily of people who have migrated there in the last thirty-five years. These individuals are mostly from outside California, although a few Indian people have come to Los Angeles from the several small reservations in southern California.

At least several hundred Indians came to Los Angeles during the 1930s and early 1940s from Oklahoma as part of the great migration of poor people from that region during the depression years. Many of their families have fared well economically, and are presently settled in the various suburban areas of Los Angeles.

In contrast, the Twin Cities (Minneapolis and St. Paul) of Minnesota have a much more homogeneous Indian population, of whom two-thirds are Chippewa, and an additional 10 percent are either Sioux, Winnebago, or Menominee. This urban area attracts Indians from a smaller geographic region, mostly Minnesota, Wisconsin, and the Dakotas.[6]

During the last twenty years, large numbers of Indians have moved to Chicago. The largest tribal groups are the Winnebago, Chippewa, Menominee, and Sioux, but there are increasing numbers from Oklahoma (five civilized tribes).

The Indian population in Chicago can be divided into three major distinguishable categories. One of these is a geographically dispersed group which is assimilating into the overall middle class population. Relatively few participate in Indian cultural activities and there is considerable intermarriage with non-Indians. This is a relatively small segment which probably does not exceed 10 percent of the Indian population.

In addition, there is an increasing number of working-class Indians. These individuals have been in the city for several years and generally are employed in semiskilled jobs such as welding, factory assembly, stockroom, and clerical office work. These persons tend to exhibit relative residential stability, and to keep their children in school until they have completed the twelfth grade.

These Indians tend to be interested in their culture, and maintain contact with relatives on the reservation either by returning annually for ceremonies or sending their children there for vacations. The American Indian Center in Chicago has been a center of activity. Although it is difficult to judge accurately the size of this group, it is probably not more than 20 percent of all Chicago Indians.[7]

The largest number of the city's Indian population can be categorized as an unstable lower working-class group which is marginal to the economy and the social structure of the metropolis. They have no residential stability; moving within the city very frequently is common. In terms of numbers, it appears that 70 percent of the Indians in Chicago belong to this category.[8]

Indian fertility is markedly higher than that of the total U.S. population, and is especially high among rural and reservation Indians. The birthrates of Indian women are, in fact, twice the rate needed to replace the Indian population in every generation. The number of children ever born among those women who have essentially completed their childbearing years (35 to 44 years of age) is 4.6 in the Indian population and 3.1 in the U.S. population.

Fertility is much higher in the rural Indian population than in the U.S. total rural population. There are 5.2 children per woman for rural nonfarm and 5.4 for rural farm Indian women, compared with 3.4 and 3.6, respectively, for all rural women.

Among urban Indians fertility per woman is 3.8 children; for the U.S. urban population it is 3. In three standard metropolitan statistical areas (SMSAs) with the largest population of Indians in 1970 the figures are comparable to those in the overall urban population: Los Angeles-Long Beach, California, 3.4; Oklahoma City, Oklahoma, 3.4; and Chicago, Illinois, 3.0.[9] This implies that Indian women who are residing in the cities have lower birthrates than those residing on reservations. Whether this is due to an attempt to limit family size on the part of urban Indian women, or reflects a tendency for women with small families to enter large cities, is impossible to determine with available data.

However, the above conclusion regarding differentials in fertility between urban and rural Indians may be far from universally true. Thus a 1972 survey among ninety-eight Omaha Indian women living in rural and urban areas of Nebraska shows that the urban experience has not depressed either fertility levels or the desire for large numbers of children. City women had more children and desired larger families than their reservation counterparts.[10]

Income

Income statistics for Indian, black and white males for 1939-1969 are presented in table 2-3.

Although the income of male Indians rose much faster than that of white males over the 1949-1969 period, the former was less than one-half the latter in 1969. The income statistics also indicate the widening gap between reservation and urban Indians. In 1949 the median income of Indians on reservations was 80 percent of that of Indians living in urban areas; in 1969 the figure had dropped to 57 percent. The increased disparity results from the migration of many relatively well-educated and highly skilled Indians from reservations to major urban centers since the late 1940s. In the metropolitan areas better paying jobs, more commensurate with their level of ability and training were available. At the same time the reservation economy remained comparatively stagnant, and as a result incomes grew slowly.

In 1970 about 33 percent of Indian families had incomes below the poverty level, compared with 11 percent for the total U.S. population. About 20 percent of urban Indian families had incomes below the poverty level in 1969; the proportion was more than twice that high among rural Indian families.[11]

From 1939 to 1969 the median income of reservation Indians grew slightly faster than the median income of black males (table 2-3). In recent years, however, the average income of black males has been double that of reservation Indians. Finally, in 1969 the median income of black males and urban male Indians was almost the same, although the latter had increased nearly three times as rapidly as the former in median income from 1949 to 1969.

There is great variation in Indian income among urban areas. In 1969 male Indians in Los Angeles-Long Beach and San Francisco-Oakland earned an annual average of $5,922 and $6,503, respectively. However, Indians in Phoenix, Arizona and Tucson, Arizona earned only an average of $3,786 and $2,731, respectively. Moreover, not all urban centers in California have relatively high earnings levels for male Indians; the average earnings of male Indians in San Diego were a modest $4,143.

There is some tendency for earnings to be higher in cities used as relocation

Table 2-3

Median Income for Male Indians, Blacks, and Whites, 1939-1969

(1969 Dollars)

Year	All Indians	Urban Indians	Reservation Indians	Blacks	Whites
1939	–	–	$ 576	$1,066	$2,035
1944	–	–	760	1,843	3,506
1949	$1,094	$1,198	950	2,218	3,780
1959	2,218	2,961	1,699	3,398	5,229
1964	–	–	2,074	3,947	6,743
1969	3,509	4,568	2,603	4,508	7,579
Percentage Increase 1939-1969	–	–	352	323	281
Percentage Increase 1949-1969	220	281	174	103	105

Source: U.S. Department of Commerce, Bureau of the Census, *Income of Families and Persons in the United States (1965), Current Population Reports* Series P-60, nos. 5, 7, and pp. 41-51 in no. 47; U.S. Department of Interior, Bureau of Indian Affairs, "Reservation Income, 1939" (Washington, D.C.: 1939), unpublished; U.S. Department of Commerce, Bureau of the Census, 1940 Census of Population, *The Labor Force* (Washington, D.C.: U.S. Government Printing Office, 1943), table 71, p. 116; U.S. Department of Commerce, Bureau of the Census, 1940 Census of Population, *Education* (Washington, D.C.: U.S. Government Printing Office, 1943), table 31, p. 161; U.S. Department of Commerce, Bureau of the Census, 1950 Census of Population, *Nonwhite Population by Race* (Washington, D.C.: U.S. Government Printing Office, 1953), table 10, p. 32 and table 21, p. 72; U.S. Department of Commerce, Bureau of the Census, 1950 Census of Population, *Occupational Characteristics* (Washington, D.C.: U.S. Government Printing Office, 1956), table 10, p. 183 and table 21, p. 215; U.S. Department of Commerce, Bureau of the Census, 1960 Census of Population, *Nonwhite Population by Race* (Washington, D.C.: U.S. Government Printing Office, 1963), table 33, p. 104; U.S. Department of Commerce, Bureau of the Census, 1960 Census of Population, *Occupational Characteristics* (Washington, D.C.: U.S. Government Printing Office, 1963), table 25, p. 296 and table 26, p. 215; U.S. Department of Interior, Bureau of Indian Affairs, "Selected Data on Indian Reservations Eligible for Designation Under Public Works and Economic Development Act" of Commerce, Bureau of the Census, 1970 Census of Population, *American Indians* (Washington, D.C.: U.S. Government Printing Office, 1973), table 13, pp. 161-163; and U.S. Department of Commerce, Bureau of the Census, 1970 Census of Population, *Education* (Washington D.C.: U.S. Government Printing Office, 1973), table 7, pp. 149-151.

Note: Data include all males and all sources of income, whether earned or unearned.

centers by the BIA as compared to other urban areas, perhaps implying that in the former the BIA has been successful in placing Indians in relatively well-paying jobs. However, other factors should be considered, such as the industrial and occupational structure of employment in the various metropolitan areas as well as the general level of wages.

The standard of living for urban Indians may not differ as much from that of reservation Indians as income levels would indicate. First, reservation Indians are entitled to comprehensive free medical care (provided by the Public Health Service, Division of Indian Health) if they are one-fourth or more Indian blood. Nonreservation Indians are not automatically entitled to such care.[a] Second, reservation Indians often reside rent free on allotted or tribal land, but urban Indians must usually pay rent for housing. Third, the cost of goods and services is higher in the urban areas with sizable Indian populations (Los Angeles, Denver, or Chicago) than on many reservations. Thus, the real income differential between reservation and urban Indians is correspondingly reduced.[b]

Changes in Income

Table 2-4 indicates changes in the income of male urban Indians from 1960-1970 for ten major centers for urban Indian population.

Table 2-4
Median Income, Urban Indian Males, Selected Cities, 1960-1970

City	Income 1960	Income 1970	Percentage Change
Oklahoma City	$2,658	$5,087	92
Los Angeles	3,423	5,690	66
Chicago	3,473	5,896	70
Minneapolis	1,978	5,366	171
Buffalo	3,712	3,996	35
Albuquerque	2,392	4,322	81
Seattle	2,321	5,439	134
San Francisco	3,349	6,175	84
New York	3,660	5,359	46
San Diego	2,070	2,854	38

Sources: U.S. Department of Commerce, Bureau of the Census, 1960 Census of Population, *Nonwhite Population by Race* (Washington, D.C.: U.S. Government Printing Office, 1963), table 26, p. 240; and U.S. Department of Commerce, Bureau of the Census, 1970 Census of Population, *American Indians* (Washington, D.C.: U.S. Government Printing Office, 1973), table 13, pp. 158-160.

[a]Low-income urban Indians are eligible to participate in the Medicaid program and elderly Indians can enroll for Medicare benefits. These individuals are extremely reluctant, however, to participate in welfare and social service programs intended for the general population. See Joan Ablon, "American Indian Relocation: Problems of Dependency and Management in the City," *Phylon* 26 (Winter 1965).

[b]On some very isolated reservations, however, where Indians must rely on purchases from trading posts, the monopoly position of the trader and substantial transportation costs have resulted in high prices.

Income growth rates were highest in Oklahoma City, Minneapolis, Seattle, and San Francisco. San Francisco, Minneapolis, and Oklahoma City are field centers for the Bureau of Indian Affairs' training and relocation programs, but the rapid growth in Indian income and population in Seattle suggests that high incomes may have attracted many Indians to this and other cities quite independently of BIA relocation and training programs.

There is little association between incomes in 1960 and incomes in 1970 by urban area. The rank correlation for the ten metropolitan areas was only 0.21. Incomes grew more slowly in cities where Indian communities had been established for many years, such as New York and Buffalo, in contrast to cities experiencing rapid migration, such as Minneapolis, Seattle, Los Angeles, and San Francisco.

Estimates have been obtained of the net outmigration of Indians from nonmetropolitan counties where they comprise the overwhelming majority of the nonwhite population and where nonwhite migration data in reality refers to Indians. These data indicate a net outmigration of about 14 percent for the Indian population alive in 1960 and surviving to 1970. Such rates are substantial, but do not approach those commonly found for nonmetropolitan blacks.[12]

Outmigration from nonmetropolitan areas has been the most substantial in the Upper Midwest, where it is estimated that more than 50 percent of the Indians reaching age twenty have departed. This is in contrast to a net outmigration of young people of only about 16 percent in Washington and Oregon. Thus, the migration pattern varies considerably among different parts of the country and from tribe to tribe.[13]

The reasons for urban Indian migration have been similar to other low income rural persons. These individuals have wanted employment and better living conditions.

Canadian Indians and Eskimos have migrated to the cities for much the same reasons. A recent survey in Toronto found the three most frequent reasons given by Indians to be employment, education, and "excitement."[14] Census data for 1951 and 1961 in Canada showed the Indian population of Toronto increasing tenfold; Winnepeg, fivefold; and Montreal, twofold during this ten-year period.[15]

Occupational Status

The distribution of the Indian labor force by occupation reveals a concentration among the lowest paying positions (table 2-5). However, the occupational status of Indians was more favorable than that of blacks, with higher proportions of the former classified as professionals, managers, and craftsmen, and with fewer enumerated as operatives, laborers, and service workers than the latter.

Nearly half of all urban Indians are employed as craftsmen and foremen or

Table 2-5
Percent Distribution of Indian, Black, and White Males by Occupation Group, 1940, 1960, and 1970

Occupation Group	Indian					Black			White		
	1940	1960	1970 Total	1970 Urban	1970 Rural	1940	1960	1970	1940	1960	1970
Professional and Technical	2.2	4.9	9.2	11.4	6.8	1.8	3.4	5.7	5.9	11.6	14.9
Managers, officials and proprietors—except farmers	1.4	2.8	5.0	5.8	4.2	1.3	1.9	2.8	10.7	12.1	12.4
Clerical and sales	2.0	4.9	8.1	7.3	3.9	2.0	7.0	10.0	14.0	15.1	14.8
Craftsmen and foremen	5.7	15.5	22.1	23.1	20.9	4.4	10.7	15.4	15.7	21.1	21.9
Operatives	6.2	21.9	23.9	25.6	22.1	12.6	26.7	29.5	18.9	20.1	18.8
Laborers	11.4	20.2	13.2	10.8	15.8	21.4	22.2	16.1	7.5	6.0	6.0
Service workers	2.6	6.3	10.4	10.8	10.1	15.3	16.0	15.9	6.0	5.7	7.3
Farmers and managers	46.7	9.5	2.3	0.2	4.6	21.2	4.7	0.9	15.1	5.8	2.8
Farm laborers	21.7	14.0	5.7	1.8	10.2	19.9	7.5	3.6	7.0	2.5	1.5

Sources: U.S. Department of Commerce, Bureau of the Census, 1940 Census of Population, *Charcteristics of the Nonwhite Population by Race* (Washington, D.C.: U.S. Government Printing Office, 1943), table 26, pp. 83-84; U.S. Department of Commerce, Bureau of the Census, 1940 Census of Population, *The Labor Force* (Washington, D.C.: U.S. Government Printing Office, 1943), table 62, pp. 88-89; U.S. Department of Commerce, Bureau of the Census, 1960 Census of Population, *Nonwhite Population by Race* (Washington, D.C.: U.S. Government Printing Office, 1963), table 33, p. 104; U.S. Department of Commerce, Bureau of the Census, 1960 Census of Population, *Occupational Characteristics* (Washington, D.C.: U.S. Government Printing Office, 1963), table 2, pp. 11-20 and table 3, pp. 21-30; U.S. Department of Commerce, Bureau of the Census, 1970 Census of Population, *American Indians* (Washington, D.C.: U.S. Government Printing Office, 1973), table 7, p. 86; and U.S. Department of Commerce, Bureau of the Census, *The Social and Economic Status of Negroes in the United States* (Washington, D.C.: U.S. Government Printing Office, 1973), table 48, p. 60.

operatives. This rapid growth in skilled and unskilled employment of Indians has been associated with the migration during the 1950s and 1960s of younger Indians from the reservations to urban centers in the West. Many of these migrants were participating in training and relocation programs operated by the Bureau of Indian Affairs.

In terms of industrial employment, nearly one-half of all urban Indians worked in the fields of manufacturing and wholesale and retail trade in 1970. This was almost identical to the proportion of the general population employed in those industries.

Educational Attainment

One of the most important factors accounting for the relatively rapid economic progress of Indian males has been the major gains in educational attainment achieved in the past generation (table 2-6).

The gap in educational attainment between reservation and urban Indian males is significant. In 1970 urban Indians twenty-five years of age and over had an average of 11.2 years of schooling compared to 8.7 years of schooling for rural (primarily reservation) Indians. One in eight rural Indians had no schooling at all compared to one in forty urban Indians. One reason for the gap in educational attainment is that urban Indians often start school earlier and have educational opportunities similar to non-Indians living in cities. Not until after the Second World War, however, were there enough facilities to permit a majority of reservation Indians to attend high school. Moreover, during the 1960s only about 55 to 60 percent of reservation students completed high school.[16] Widespread poverty and lack of economic opportunity on the reservations reduce the incentive to complete secondary school, since the underdeveloped reservation economy provides few jobs for either high school graduates or dropouts.

Another factor accounting for the gap in educational attainment between urban and reservation Indians is the migration of better educated native Americans from rural to metropolitan areas. Some direct evidence of the latter phenomenon can be found by comparing the educational attainment of participants in BIA manpower programs with nonparticipants of comparable age. The difference between the median years of schooling for those participating in the direct relocation program and nonparticipants was nearly two years, while the difference in average schooling levels between those receiving vocational training and nontrainees was more than three years.[17] However, 75 percent of the courses taken by the vocational trainees require a minimum of high school graduation prior to enrollment.[c] Thus, the high educational level of the trainees reflects the requirements of the program as well as the tendency for the better-educated Indian to avail himself of training opportunities.

---

[c]There is no educational requirement for participation in the direct-relocation program.

Table 2-6
Percent Distribution of Indian, Black, and White Males by Years of School Completed, 1940, 1960, and 1970

Years of School Completed	Indian 1940	Indian 1960	Indian 1970 Total	Indian 1970 Urban	Indian 1970 Rural	Black 1940	Black 1960	Black 1970	White 1940	White 1960	White 1970
0	23.9	9.6	7.7	2.7	12.3	8.1	5.0	2.2	1.2	0.9	0.7
1-4	20.1	12.6	7.7	5.2	10.1	33.4	17.7	10.1	5.5	3.8	2.3
5-8	38.7	37.8	28.0	23.8	31.8	41.2	36.2	27.4	42.2	28.9	19.9
9-11	9.6	22.8	23.3	24.8	21.9	9.9	22.7	25.1	20.0	20.2	20.5
12	4.9	11.6	22.0	26.9	17.6	4.6	12.1	23.2	18.4	24.8	31.5
13-15	2.0	4.0	7.5	10.8	4.5	1.8	4.0	6.9	7.0	9.8	10.6
16 or more	0.7	1.6	3.8	5.9	1.8	1.1	2.2	5.2	5.8	11.6	14.5
Median	5.5	8.4	9.8	11.2	8.7	5.3	8.3	10.2	8.7	12.2	12.3

Sources: U.S. Department of Commerce, Bureau of the Census, 1940 Census of Population, *Characteristics of the Nonwhite Population by Race* (Washington, D.C.: U.S. Government Printing Office, 1943), table 24, p. 80; U.S. Department of Commerce, Bureau of the Census, 1940 Census of Population, *Educational Attainment by Economic Characteristics and Marital Status* (Washington, D.C.: U.S. Government Printing Office, 1943), table 17, p. 75 and table 18, p. 82; U.S. Department of Commerce, Bureau of the Census, 1960 Census of Population, *Nonwhite Population by Race* (Washington, D.C.: U.S. Government Printing Office, 1963), table 9, p. 9 and table 10, p. 12; U.S. Department of Commerce, Bureau of the Census, 1960 Census of Population, *Educational Attainment* (Washington, D.C.: U.S. Government Printing Office, 1963), table 1, p. 1; U.S. Department of Commerce, Bureau of the Census, 1970 Census of Population, *American Indians* (Washington, D.C.: U.S. Government Printing Office, 1973), table 5, pp. 36-39; and U.S. Department of Commerce, Bureau of the Census, 1970 Census of Population, *Educational Attainment* (Washington, D.C.: U.S. Government Printing Office, 1973), table 5, pp. 104 and 106.

A recent study of American Indian migration to Los Angeles confirms these results. The median years of schooling of the male migrants was 11.2 years or about three years more than that of male nonmigrants of similar age from the same tribes.[18]

From 1940 to 1970 the educational attainment of Indians and blacks has been comparable. However, urban Indians averaged nearly one year more formal education than urban blacks and one year less schooling than urban whites in 1970. Moreover, urban Indians 20-34 years of age averaged 12.2 years of schooling—about the same as urban whites of comparable age. In addition, school enrollment rates of young urban Indians are comparable to that of urban whites. Thus, the burden of poor education is primarily carried by the older Indians.

However, one of the most important educational concerns regarding Indians is the low rate of college attendance and completion. Only 17 percent of the eligible eighteen-year-old Indian population attend college as opposed to 38 percent of the general population. Only one-fourth of those Indians who enroll in college will graduate.[19]

Manpower Utilization

The very low levels of Indian income are associated with unemployment rates several times those of non-Indians (see table 2-7).

While the unemployment rates for blacks and whites fell sharply between 1940 and 1960, the rate for Indians rose 16 percent. This increase was chiefly a result of the great exodus of Indians from agriculture in search of better paid employment. Since many of them lacked training and education, they were restricted to unskilled occupations with high rates of joblessness, particularly in reservation areas where there had been little industrialization.

Some of the discrepancy between unemployment rates for reservation Indians and other groups is a matter of definition. Although the Department of Labor considers as unemployed only those willing and able to work who are not employed, the BIA considers an individual who is able but unwilling to work as unemployed. This raises the unemployment rate for reservation Indians above the level that would prevail if the standard Department of Labor definition of unemployment were used.

Nonreservation Indians have unemployment rates 10-15 percent higher than blacks. Both populations are highly urbanized (with 70 percent of all blacks living in urban areas and over 90 percent of nonreservation Indians), and have roughly similar employment and income levels. Many of the reservation Indians newly arrived in cities have adjustment problems very similar to those of southern blacks who have migrated to a northern urban center.

Between 1950 and 1970 the unemployment rate for nonreservation Indians

21

Table 2-7
Unemployment Rates, Indian, Black, and White Males, Selected Years, 1940-1975
(in percent)

Year	Indians			Blacks	Whites
	All	*Urban*	*Reservation*		
1940	32.9	–	–	18.0	14.8
1950	–	15.1	–	9.6	5.9
1958	–	–	43.5	13.8	6.1
1960	38.2	12.1	51.3	10.7	4.8
1962	–	–	43.4	10.9	4.6
1965	–	–	41.9	7.4	3.6
1967	–	–	37.3	6.0	2.7
1970	28.6	9.4	41.0	8.2	4.0
1972	–	–	40.0	10.0	4.5
1975	–	–	39.8	13.7	7.2

Sources: U.S. Department of Labor, *Manpower Report of the President, 1973* (Washington, D.C.: U.S. Government Printing Office, 1973), p. 145; U.S. Department of Commerce, Bureau of the Census, 1940 Census of Population, *Characteristics of the Nonwhite Population by Race* (Washington, D.C.: U.S. Government Printing Office, 1943), table 25, p. 82; U.S. Department of Commerce, Bureau of the Census, 1940 Census of Population, *The Labor Force* (Washington, D.C.: U.S. Government Printing Office, 1943), table 4, p. 18; U.S. Department of Commerce, Bureau of the Census, 1950 Census of Population, *Nonwhite Population by Race* (Washington, D.C.: U.S. Government Printing Office, 1953), table 10, p. 32; U.S. Department of Commerce, Bureau of the Census, 1960 Census of Population, *Nonwhite Population by Race* (Washington, D.C.: U.S. Government Printing Office, 1963), table 33, p. 104; U.S. Department of Interior, Bureau of Indian Affairs, *Indian Unemployment Survey* (Washington, D.C.: U.S. Government Printing Office, 1963); U.S. Department of Interior, Bureau of Indian Affairs, unpublished tabulation (December 1967); U.S. Department of Interior, Bureau of Indian Affairs, "Estimates of Resident Indian Population and Labor Force Status, by State and Reservation, March 1972" (Washington, D.C.: U.S. Department of Interior, 1973), mimeographed; and U.S. Department of Interior, Bureau of Indian Affairs, "Estimates of Resident Indian Population and Labor Force Status, by State and Reservation, April 1975" (Washington, D.C.: U.S. Department of Interior, 1975), mimeographed.

Note: Data for Indians in all years and blacks and whites in 1940 include those 14 years old and over; all other data include males 16 years old and over.

fell by nearly 40 percent in spite of a major migration from the reservation to urban areas. This reflects some tendency for migrants to enter cities with relatively tight labor markets.

Among the cities with large Indian populations unemployment in 1970 among male urban Indians ranged from 3.8 percent in Dallas and 4.3 in Chicago (actually below the U.S. average) to 18.0 percent in Seattle. In general, unemployment was lowest among urban Indians residing in Oklahoma, Texas, New Mexico, and Arizona, and highest among urban Indians located in

Minnesota, Washington, and Oregon. California, the state with the largest number of urban Indians, occupied an intermediate position with respect to unemployment rates.

Housing

One of the biggest problems that a newly arrived Indian faces in the city is to obtain adequate housing at a price that is affordable. Most urban Indians initially tend to cluster in the central cities, where housing costs are lowest, and then to gradually move elsewhere within the metropolitan area as economic circumstances improve. Census data permit a comparison of the total U.S. urban population, the urban Indian population, and the urban black population in terms of a number of selected characteristics of housing quality (table 2-8).

As indicated above, urban Indians have significantly lower housing quality than that of the general population in terms of most of the characteristics listed. However, in spite of the poor quality of housing for Indians in urban areas, they still must spend nearly one-fourth of their incomes on housing.

Although the quality of housing for urban Indians is far below that of the white urban population, it is considerably better than rural Indian housing. For example, in 1970, 46 percent of all rural Indian housing had inadequate plumbing facilities compared to 8 percent for urban Indians, and 15 percent for

Table 2-8
Housing Quality, Selected Characteristics for Urban Indians, Blacks, and All Races

Characteristic	Indians	Blacks	All Races
Percentage owner occupied	38.6	34.3	58.4
Lacking some plumbing facilities	8.0	3.0	2.5
Median value of home	$13,500	$12,700	$19,000
Median monthly rent	$81	$98	$120
Percentage of income allocated for rent	23.0	21.0	17.0

Sources: U.S. Department of Commerce, Bureau of the Census, Census of Housing, *Housing of Selected Racial Groups* (Washington, D.C.: U.S. Government Printing Office, 1973), table A-1, p. 1; and U.S. Department of Commerce, Bureau of the Census, 1970 Census of Housing, *Housing Characteristics by Household Composition* (Washington, D.C.: U.S. Government Printing Office, 1973), table A, p. 4 and table B, p. 7.

the white rural population. The mean value of rural Indian housing was only $5,000 compared to $13,500 for urban Indians, and $12,900 for the U.S. rural population. Finally, 19 percent of urban Indian housing is considered crowded (more than one resident per room), compared to 44 percent for rural Indians, and 10 percent for the U.S. rural population.

Summary

The American Indian population is increasing more rapidly than that of any minority group and presently numbers approximately one million. Roughly half of this population now resides in metropolitan areas compared to slightly more than one-fourth in 1960.

In terms of labor force status, income, and housing, reservation Indians are the most disadvantaged group in the United States. Urban Indians have an economic status which is comparable to blacks.

Over time the economic position of the urban Indian has improved relative to his reservation counterpart. This reflects the comparative stagnation of the reservation economy and the rapid growth in employment opportunities for Indians who have migrated to urban centers. Many of the latter have participated in training and relocation programs operated by the BIA.

Notes

1. U.S. Department of Interior, Bureau of Indian Affairs, "Answers to Questions About American Indians" (Washington, D.C.: U.S. Government Printing Office, 1965), p. 2.

2. Nampeo D.R. McKenney and Karen A. Crook, "Census Data and Native Americans," in Jerry McDonald and Tony Lazewski, eds., *Geographical Perspectives on Native Americans: Topics and Resources*, no. 1 (Washington, D.C.: Association of American Geographers, 1976), p. 179.

3. Calvin Beale, "Migration Patterns of Minorities in the United States," *American Journal of Agricultural Economics* 55, no. 5 (December 1973):944.

4. Institute for Government Research, *The Problem of Indian Administration* (Baltimore: The Johns Hopkins Press, 1928), p. 346.

5. John A. Price, "The Migration and Adaptation of American Indians to Los Angeles," *Human Organization*, 27, no. 2 (Summer 1968):168-175.

6. Murray Wax, *Indian Americans: Unity and Diversity* (Englewood Cliffs: Prentice-Hall, 1971), p. 159.

7. Estelle Fuchs and Robert Havighurst, *To Live on This Earth: American Indian Education* (New York: Doubleday, 1972), p. 109.

8. Ibid., pp. 107-109.

9. Helen Johnson, *American Indians in Transition*, Agricultural Economic Report no. 283 (Washington, D.C.: U.S. Department of Agriculture, Economic Research Service, April 1975), p. 5.

10. Margo Liberty, David Hughey, and Richard Scoglion, "Rural and Urban Omaha Indian Fertility," *Human Biology* 48, no. 1 (February 1976):59.

11. Johnson, *American Indians in Transition*, p. 7.

12. Beale, "Migration Patterns of Minorities," p. 944.

13. Johnson, *American Indians in Transition*, p. 5.

14. Mark Nagler, *Indians in the City: A Study of the Urbanization of Indians in Toronto* (Ottawa: Canadian Research Center for Anthropology, St. Paul University, 1970).

15. Fuchs and Havighurst, *To Live on This Earth*, p. 275.

16. Alphonse D. Selinger, *The American Indian High School Dropout: The Magnitude of the Problem* (Washington, D.C.: Office of Education, 1968); and Charles S. Owens and Willard P. Bass, *The American Indian High School Dropout in the Southwest* (Washington, D.C.: Office of Education, 1969).

17. U.S. Department of Interior, Bureau of Indian Affairs, "A Follow-Up Study of 1963 Recipients of the Services of the Employment Assistance Program" (Washington, D.C.: Bureau of Indian Affairs, 1968), mimeographed.

18. Price, "Migration and Adaptation of American Indians," pp. 168-175. This study included all migrated Indians and not only those who participated in Bureau of Indian Affairs' relocation programs.

19. U.S. Office of Education, Office of Indian Education, *The Indian Education Act of 1972: Report of Progress for the Third Year of the Program*, DHEW Publication No. (OE) 76-02401 (Washington, D.C.: U.S. Government Printing Office, 1976), p. I-1.

3 Manpower and Relocation Programs

The first mass migration of Indians from the reservations occurred during the Second World War. Some twenty-three thousand men served in the Armed Forces; this was 32 percent of all able-bodied male Indians between eighteen and fifty years of age (some eight hundred women also served). An undetermined number did not return to the reservations after the war, but remained in urban centers.

In addition, forty-six thousand Indians left the reservations in 1943 to obtain wartime employment. About half of them went into industry where manpower shortages were severe, and the other half into agricultural occupations. Another forty-four thousand left the reservation in 1944.[1] After the war most of those in defense-related industries were laid off, and a large proportion returned to the reservations. In 1948 the Bureau of Indian Affairs established a program of job placement services for Navajos, many of whom were engaged in seasonal farm and railroad track work.[2] The BIA worked closely with the Arizona and New Mexico State Employment Services and the Railroad Retirement Board in expanding employment opportunities for Navajos in Arizona, New Mexico, and Salt Lake City, Utah, where sizeable groups of Indians were living.

Direct Relocation

In the fall of 1950 the bureau launched a full-scale relocation program for Indians who desired permanent employment away from the reservations. Field or placement offices were established in several cities and are still operating in Chicago, Cleveland, Dallas, Denver, Los Angeles, Oakland, San Francisco, and San Jose (California). In 1968 two smaller centers were opened in Oklahoma in Tulsa and Oklahoma City.

The first applicants were placed in February 1952, and by 1972 (when the emphasis of the program changed significantly), the program had relocated more than 100,000 persons, including dependents (see table 3-1).

An impetus to the BIA relocation program was the desire on the part of Congress to terminate services provided to the reservation Indian by the federal government. In 1953 Congress passed a termination resolution and several tribes were terminated with disastrous results. The feeling that past programs had kept the Indian in a dependent or wardship status was contrasted to the possibilities

Table 3-1
Participants and Funding of Employment Assistance Programs, 1952-1978

Year	Direct Employment		Adult Vocational Training	
	Participants	Expenditures	Participants	Expenditures
1952	442	$ 576,480	–	$ –
1956	2,083	991,617	–	–
1960	1,798	2,732,663	936	3,073,751
1964	1,985	2,747,000	1,805	6,673,000
1968	2,928	7,267,000	3,172	13,830,000
1970	3,591	12,761,000	3,935	25,000,000
1972	6,378[a]	15,133,000	4,802[b]	24,716,000
1974	6,590	13,336,849	4,929	20,882,000
1975	7,018	14,107,000	3,715	19,276,000
1976	6,400	11,480,400	3,134	20,103,500
1977	5,911	11,310,000[c]	3,204	19,800,000
1978	5,870	11,295,000	2,700	18,061,000

Sources: U.S. Department of Interior, Bureau of Indian Affairs, "Statistical Summary of Activities from Inception of Program Through June 30, 1975," unpublished tabulation; U.S. Department of Interior, Bureau of Indian Affairs, Division of Employment Assistance, "Funds Appropriated Under the Programs of Relocation and Adult Vocational Training Services," unpublished tabulation, 1976; U.S. Department of Interior, Bureau of Indian Affairs, "Budget Justification Estimates, Fiscal Year, 1978," (Washington, D.C.: Bureau of Indian Affairs, 1977), IA 36-43, mimeographed.

[a]The large increase from 1970-1972 is accounted for by the considerable number of persons found jobs on or near the reservation.

[b]The increase in the number of trainees reflects a growth in the number trained and found jobs on or near the reservation.

[c]Estimated.

of assimilation and financial independence to be found in urban areas. Moreover, it was widely believed that Indian reservations were overpopulated with a considerable quantity of surplus labor. To quote a 1954 Congressional report: "Most of the reservations are greatly overpopulated, and could not support the present population at anything approaching a reasonably adequate American standard of living. Past studies indicate that the resources of many reservations, when fully developed, could support no more than 60 percent of the current population, and the Indian population is increasing rapidly."[3]

To participate in the direct employment program, an Indian files an application with an employment assistance officer on or near the reservation. The officer ascertains the Indian's work preferences, then refers him to the state employment service for aptitude testing (usually the General Aptitude Test battery). The employment officer discusses the results of the examination with the applicant and counsels him on the conditions he will encounter after relocation.

Because the Indians who apply for direct relocation are usually unable to defray the cost of moving, the Bureau of Indian Affairs has established various kinds of assistance to ease the financial burden.[4] These include a medical examination for the whole family; transportation for the family to the place of employment; low cost temporary housing; housewares, including furniture; additional counseling and advice in job seeking.

The field office staff follows up the applicant for one year after placement, providing counseling and additional job placement services if he leaves his first position. Eligibility for grants is limited after the initial relocation.

The program is completely voluntary. According to Indian leaders as well as BIA personnel, the bureau does not pressure Indians in any way to apply for relocation.

Adult Vocational Training

Partly because so few Indians were employed in positions above the unskilled category, the Indian Vocational Training Act of 1956 provides for a wide variety of courses for reservation Indians. By 1972 there were available 2,063 approved courses at 666 accredited vocational schools located both in urban centers and near reservations.[5] However, most graduates eventually move to urban areas, regardless of where they have taken their training.

Applicants for vocational training (AVT) must generally be between the ages of eighteen and thirty-five. Preference is given to unemployed or under-employed applicants who need training to obtain satisfactory jobs.[6] Eligibility for the various courses depends on the educational requirements of the occupation and vary from eight to twelve years of schooling.

The BIA pays for the trainee's and his family's transportation to the place of training and subsistence enroute; subsistence during the course of training; and tuition, books, supplies, and tools used in training. Upon completion of the vocational course the enrollee receives job placement services including transportation, moving expenses, and housing assistance that are provided on the same basis as in the direct relocation program. From 1958 to 1972 the program grew steadily from 397 participants in 1958 to 4,802 in 1972 (table 3-1). A total of 37,517 persons were enrolled in courses during that fourteen-year period.

Recipients of employment assistance services tended to be young and better educated than nonparticipating individuals of comparable age.[a] Although males and single individuals predominate, there is a sizable minority of women participants. Nine of every ten enrollees were unemployed when they applied for services. Moreover, the few who were employed held low paying jobs. Some descriptive features of enrollees are presented in table 3-2.

---

[a]The median years of schooling of all reservation Indians 18-35 was between nine and ten years in 1970.

Table 3-2

Selected Characteristics of Individuals Receiving BIA Employment Services, 1970-1971

(in percent unless otherwise indicated)

	Direct Employment	Adult Vocational Training
Male	76.0	58.0
Female	24.0	42.0
Single	63.0	72.0
Family	37.0	28.0
Average size of family	4.1	3.4
Average age	23.0	27.0
Median years of school	10.6	12.0
On welfare at time of application	20.0	14.0
Unemployed at time of application	93.0	90.0

Sources: U.S. Department of Interior, Bureau of Indian Affairs, "Annual Statistical Summary, 1971," mimeographed; U.S. Department of Interior, Bureau of Indian Affairs, "Federal Manpower Programs, Agency Summary 50A," unpublished report, 1972.

Evaluation

There are a variety of dimensions of program effectiveness that must be considered in evaluating manpower programs. One important factor used to assess program effectiveness is the change in the earnings levels of those participating in the program in comparison to what they previously earned.[b] The change in economic status is one of the important benefits of the program.

Another factor to be considered is the change in the employment status of participants as a result of the education and training received. Hopefully, the program should result in a reduction of the proportion of individuals who were unemployed or not in the labor force and an increase in the proportion with full-time, year-round employment. In addition, one would hope that the occupational status of those trainees who were employed prior to training would be enhanced.

A third measure of efficiency is the proportion of trainees who actually complete the program. It is likely that a brief experience with a manpower program leaves little lasting benefit. One might expect that a project exclusively serving a disadvantaged clientele would have a higher dropout rate than one in which the enrollees were skilled, experienced workers. Therefore, a comparison

[b]Another method is to compare the earnings of the participants over time with those of a control group (a comparable group of workers who did not receive program services). The higher earnings of the program enrollees, in comparison to the control group, serve as a measure of program effectiveness.

of noncompletion rates would not be particularly meaningful. However, one can usefully compare the dropout rates for programs with the same length of training that serve similar kinds of clients.

A fourth aspect of manpower assessment is the percentage of participants who obtain jobs related to the training they have acquired. This is a function not only of the quality of training received, but the effectiveness of the placement service as well as follow-up efforts. Moreover, successful placement also depends on general economic conditions. It is more difficult to place graduates in training-related jobs during recession than prosperity.

A final effect of a manpower program is its effect on the social adjustment of participants. For example, do participants experience a significant decline in arrest rates in comparison to the period prior to enrollment?

Two major evaluations of Indian manpower programs have been based on a sample of 121 relocatees and 170 native Americans who had received adult vocational training prior to employment. Services were received in 1963 and a considerable quantity of data regarding the social and economic status of these individuals in 1964-1966 was obtained by the Bureau of Indian Affairs in a national survey. This data was never analyzed by the BIA. However, academic social scientists have examined these data for the purposes of program evaluation.

Some effects of urban relocation are indicated in the comparison of pre- and post-relocation experiences presented in table 3-3. Participants in both direct employment and adult vocational training showed significant increases in economic adjustment. Following relocation the number of months of employ-

Table 3-3
Pre- and Post-Relocation Economic Status of Indian Migrants Participating in Adult Vocational Training and Direct Employment Programs During 1963

	1960-1962	1964-1966
Direct Employment		
Income	$1,050	$2,690
Employment (months)	13.9	22.4
Housing (percent substandard)	63	28
Adult Vocational Training		
Income	$1,280	$3,320
Employment (months)	10.2	20.8
Housing (percent substandard)	74	44

Sources: Data from Alan Sorkin, American Indians and Federal Aid (Washington, D.C.: The Brookings Institution, 1971), p. 216; Lawrence Clinton, Bruce A. Chadwick, and Howard M. Bahr, "Urban Relocation Reconsidered: Antecedents of Employment Among Indian Males," *Rural Sociology* 40, no. 2 (Spring 1975), p. 125.

ment nearly doubled, income increased more dramatically, and the number of respondents living in substandard housing decreased substantially.

The above findings indicate that urban relocation significantly improved migrants' economic status. However, off-reservation residence results in the loss of free Public Health Service medical and dental care as well as increased housing and food expenses. Thus, it could be argued that the apparent income differential merely offsets the higher costs of living in the city. The BIA national survey contained a question regarding the standard of living before and after relocation. Thus, 32 percent of the direct employment participants reported they were living "much better," another 32 percent reported being "somewhat better," 32 percent felt things were "about the same," and only 2 percent reported that "things were worse." The distribution of responses by adult vocational training participants was comparable: 39 percent said they were doing "much better," 31 percent "somewhat better," 24 percent "about the same," and only 5 percent "worse." Thus, despite the higher cost of living in cities, an overwhelming majority of the participants of both manpower programs said that their economic condition had improved as a consequence of relocation.[7]

Graves and Lave relate a variety of background factors of 259 male Navajo Indian migrants to their starting wages in Denver. The major determinants of the latter are years of education beyond ten, highest wage earned prior to migration, whether or not the migrant had received skilled vocational training, whether he was married, and whether his father had spent a majority of his time as a wage laborer. No economic indices of the state of the job market at the time of the migrant's arrival in Denver bore any relationship to his starting wage. However, it is speculated that differential employer attitudes toward Indians as well as the varying skills of BIA job placement officers are probably important external variables.[8]

Characteristics Linked to Post-Migration Employment

An inverse relationship between degree of Indian ancestry and employment has been reported among Indian migrants in Dallas and in the Midwest.[9] Ancestry can be relevant for two reasons. First, it may indicate a degree of assimilation or acculturation; persons with little or no white ancestry may have had insufficient opportunity to learn the attitudes and customs that foster adjustment to the dominant culture of an industrial society. Also, a high degree of Indian ancestry may mean that one's racial identity is readily visible to potential employers and thus becomes a basis for discrimination.

At least two studies suggest that age is directly related to occupational adjustment and stable urban residence.[10] Apparently young migrants have greater difficulty obtaining employment and are less likely to remain in the city.

Employment experience prior to relocation was found to be an important factor explaining economic adjustment of Navajos in Denver where premigration work experience was related to the level of the starting wage.[11] The level of prior income is related to previous employment experience. The Denver study also found a significant relationship between the highest wage an Indian had earned prior to migration and his starting wage in Denver.[12]

Excessive drinking is also related to adjustment problems in the city. Two studies have linked postrelocation drinking to unemployment.[13] While these findings do not distinguish whether alcoholism is the cause or effect of unemployment, it seems likely that problem drinking prior to relocation predisposes one to similar difficulties in the city and, thus reduces the likelihood of finding and holding a job.

Moreover, an arrest record before leaving home has been shown to have negative consequences for urban employment.[14] After relocation, arrests for alcohol-related offenses have been found to be associated with unemployment.[15] The importance of premigration arrests is that illegal behavior may reflect social background and personality characteristics which limit occupational adjustment. Also an arrest record may make it harder for a migrant to get a job in the first place.

Marital status has been shown to have a strong relationship to migrant employment. Married individuals have demonstrated higher performance in both training and occupational endeavors. Thus, in Denver a higher proportion of married than single migrants were employed. Similar results were found in the Pacific Northwest. Moreover, married trainees had a higher rate of vocational course completion.[16] Perhaps a spouse and children provide emotional support and additional motivation for the migrant experiencing frustration in finding or keeping a job.

Finally, vocational training itself has been shown to be directly related to the occupational success of Indian migrants. Vocational training is positively associated with the probability of finding and holding a job and with the level of starting salary.[17]

However, for the relocatees receiving vocational training, *the length of training* (number of months completed) was only slightly related to the number of months of postrelocation employment ($r = .13$). In other words, whether one was preparing for skilled or semiskilled work had little effect on employment stability. Welders and barbers were able to find and keep jobs as readily as TV repairmen and electronics specialists.

Moreover, years of school emerged as an important predictor of employment for participants in the direct employment program but not for those receiving adult vocational training. This suggests that, when vocational training is provided, previous education becomes somewhat irrelevant as a determinant of subsequent employment. However, for those relocated without training the amount of education completed had an impact on length of employment.[18]

Dropout Rates

A study by Clinton, Chadwick, and Bahr focusing on Indians participating in the adult vocational training program from several Northwest states obtained the following conclusions: males were much more likely to complete training than females (79 percent versus 47 percent).[19] Moreover, previous employment experience was the single most important factor associated with successful completion of training. Marital status, off-reservation living experience, and the BIA field interviewers' assessment prior to program participation were positively related to training completion for males. However, the effect of these latter factors was slight. For females off-reservation employment experience was the strongest factor associated with completion of training.

Nationally about 65 percent of the participants in the adult vocational training program have completed training. This compares very favorably to the reported completion rates for other federal vocational training programs such as the Manpower Development Training Program (67 percent), Job Corps (44 percent), or the Work Incentive Program (41 percent).[20] In view of the uniquely disadvantaged status of the target population—rural reservation Indians with limited education and off-reservation work experience—the high success rate of the adult vocational training program is a major achievement.

Employment Related to Training

Of those adult vocational trainees receiving services in 1963 (national sample), 61 percent were in employment related to training in 1966 and 59 percent in 1968.[21] This is a higher proportion in training-related employment than was found in an intensive survey of persons participating in the Manpower Development and Training Act Program. In the latter, only 34 percent of participants were in training-related positions 18 months after training.[22]

These results are similar to the findings of Clinton, Chadwick, and Bahr, who found that 70 percent of those participating in the adult vocational program in several Northwest states obtained training-related employment. Among those who completed the program, the percentage in training-related employment was 91 percent.[23]

Reservation Returnees

A large proportion of participants in the employment assistance programs operated by the Bureau of Indian Affairs return to their reservations. This does not necessarily indicate a failure to adjust to urban living. The Indian may return because of expanded employment opportunities on the reservation. However, the great earnings differential between migrants who remain in urban areas and those who return to the reservation (table 3-3) indicates that most who return suffer an income loss.

The Bureau of Indian Affairs maintained statistics from 1953 through 1957 which showed that three out of ten who were relocated returned home during the same fiscal year in which they migrated.[24] The data do not indicate how many Indians *eventually* returned to the reservation, a figure that would undoubtedly be much higher.

In 1958 the U.S. comptroller general's annual report criticized the BIA for maintaining inadequate statistics on various activities including the relocation program. The bureau's response to this criticism was to eliminate, in 1959, its statistical series on the status (returnee or nonreturnee) of Indians; it concluded that statistics on returnees were furnishing ammunition to critics of the program.

There is apparently great variation in returnee rates by tribe. A study of the Salt River reservation in Arizona showed that in the years 1960 through 1964, 97 percent of those relocated returned to the reservation.[25] However, only 20 percent of migrants returned to the Yakima reservation in Washington.[26]

A BIA study showed that about 37 percent of the Navajos between 1952 and 1961 later returned to the reservation, a percentage that remained fairly constant over the years.[27] However, a survey of Navajos relocating in Denver found that 50 percent of the Indians moved back to the reservation within a three-month period. The Denver Navajos only had an average of 8.5 years of schooling.[28] Weppner criticized the BIA for overselling the relocation program in that city. He maintains that because federal funds were allocated for relocation, the BIA made every effort to spend the money irrespective of the chances for successful urban adjustment.

A study of relocated Southern Plains Indians indicates only a 15 percent returnee rate within one year. There is evidence of careful selection of participants in this case.[29] Finally, a survey among the Shoshone-Bannocks on the Fort Hall reservation in Idaho showed that 80 percent of the relocatees returned to the reservation.[30]

These statistics appear to indicate that the cultural patterns of some tribes make it more difficult for their members to adjust to an urban environment. If this is true, the extension of special follow-up services to migrants from the tribes that show persistently high returnee rates may prove feasible. However, the above statistics also indicate that urban employment is not best for all program applicants.

Reasons for Returning

There has been limited research undertaken concerning *why* relocated Indians return home. The results of two studies are indicated in table 3-4.

Table 3-4
Reasons for Leaving the Relocation Area

	Navajo 1952-1964 (percent)	Southern Plains Indians 1968-1972 (percent)
Medical reasons	23	9
Alcoholism	18	16
Military service	8	2
Personal reasons	31	35
Economic reasons	19	37

Source: Paul Brinker and Benjamin Taylor, "Southern Plains Indian Relocation Returnees," *Human Organization* 33, no. 2 (Summer 1974), p. 141

Generally, returnees seem to make rational economic decisions regarding whether to remain in urban areas without free medical services; or to return home, where free services are available, but wages are relatively lower. In fact, if one's health is sufficiently poor, he might be better off receiving welfare payments plus free health services on the reservation than working in the city. Real income would actually be higher in the former situation. The federal government should consider providing health services at low cost for Indians in urban areas to prevent their returning home solely to obtain free medical care.

A large number of those who left the relocation city for personal reaons (see table 3-4) were single women relocatees who married and left with their husbands. The permanency of relocation could be improved if only males were relocated.

Of those Southern Plains Indian returnees who left for economic reasons most either could not find work or lost their jobs. Brinker and Taylor indicate that better screening prior to relocation might have reduced the number returning for economic reasons.[31] Certainly sending construction workers to urban areas in the spring rather than the fall would result in fewer returnees.

Weppner, focusing on Navajos in Denver, found that four economic variables were predictive of the Navajos' adjustment to the city. Two of the measures were found to have been influential on the reservation and two were of importance in Denver. On the reservation, the more work experience one had prior to relocation and the better one's performance in vocational training, the more likely the Navajos were to remain in Denver. If they received a job in Denver quickly and it paid relatively well, the Navajos were also more likely to remain there. One of Weppner's conclusions was that: "The Navajo who failed to adjust to Denver might have succeeded if he had had adequate vocational training." It should be added that the three factors cited by Weppner—stability in the labor market, quickness in finding a job, and the rate of pay—are all positively related to an individual's education and training.[32]

In a study of Navajo relocation, Cullum pointed out that "the only sharply positive findings ... [are] related to attendance at public school and previous occupational experience at skilled trades. Definitely negative findings emerged with regard to families containing five or more children, to heads of families over forty, and in lesser degree to persons completing less than four grades of school. The person using alcoholic beverage 'to excess' did poorly."[33]

Chadwick and White, instead of considering the decision to stay or leave the city, examined the factors which have affected the total amount of time one has lived in urban areas.[34] Focusing on Indians living in the city of Spokane, Washington and on the Spokane reservation they found that noneconomic factors, namely degree of Indian ancestry and Indian self-identification or acceptance of white culture, were respectively negatively and positively related to Indian people's migration to the city and continued residence in an urban setting. Economic variables such as employment, income, education, or housing were unimportant.

These results contradict most other studies of Indian migration to urban areas which emphasize economic considerations. For example, Graves and Van Arsdale in their study of the Navajo in Denver stressed that "only the substantial economic advantages of life in the city keep them there."[35] They do acknowledge the importance of noneconomic factors in enticing the migrant to return to the reservation and suggest that changes for the worse in economic conditions in the city or improvement on the reservation would tend to cause a return to the latter. The major discrepancies between Graves' and Van Arsdale's findings and those of Chadwick and White probably result from differences in the dependent variables examined. It should be stressed that in Graves' study the dependent variable was current residence, while in the Chadwick study the focus was upon continued urban residence regardless of where respondents lived at the time of the interview.

An alternative explanation of the different findings of the Graves and Chadwick studies is that the former studied Navajos in Denver, while the latter studied Spokanes in Spokane. The importance of tribal differences in understanding urban versus reservation residence is sufficiently great to warrant additional research.

The Chadwick and White results imply that regardless of the economic opportunities available in the city, the nonacculturated individuals who attempt to take advantage of those opportunities are likely to remain in urban areas only a short period of time. Thus, individuals and agencies interested in assisting relocating Indians "must focus upon acculturation (preparing the Indian to perceive himself as one who belongs and who is willing to interact with whites on an intimate level) at least as strongly as upon economic factors, such as the availability of employment or training."[36]

Changes in Behavior

As indicated previously one of the potential noneconomic benefits of a manpower program for the disadvantaged is a decline in antisocial behavior, which may be measured by examining arrest records. Indians seem prone to arrest. For example, police records in Denver indicate that about half of the Navajo migrants were arrested at least once during their stay in the city, with about 95 percent of the arrests alcohol-related.[37] If Indians show a decrease in arrests after participating in a manpower program, it seems reasonable to conclude that the program has reduced antisocial behavior. A comparison of the numbers in the 1963 national sample arrested before and after taking part in the manpower programs showed a substantial decline.[38] (See table 3-5.)

The decrease in arrests for vocational trainees is smaller than those relocated without training. This is probably not because of economic factors, since the former earn more money and are less subject to unemployment than the latter. Perhaps the pressure placed on the vocational trainees in their skilled and semiskilled positions (untrained migrants in unskilled positions may be less subject to pressure) led the trainees to turn to alcohol and resulted in the subsequent arrests.[39]

Beginning in 1972 there has been a redirection in the manpower programs operated by the Bureau of Indian Affairs. Since that time only about 25-30 percent of the persons entering the programs have been placed in off-reservation urban areas with the remainder placed on or near the reservation.[40] This change in focus is controversial. Job placement close to home is certainly likely to reduce the adjustment problems of the participants, who often find a hostile, alien environment in the cities. In fact, the high returnee rate has been used to justify the new policy. Moreover, it is less costly to place an applicant in a job on or near the reservation than to transport him to a distant urban area where a full-time staff is required for placement and follow-up. With placement close to home, the reservation employment assistance officer can maintain contact with the individual and provide follow-up services.

However, the range of employment opportunities and the level of earnings in jobs located on or near reservations is far below that found in the urban centers where participants have been sent for job placement. Since many enrollees in these programs are known to change jobs frequently, this behavior will be more likely to result in long-term unemployment if practiced in a reservation as opposed to an urban setting. Moreover, there is considerable evidence that the intensity of prejudice and discrimination against Indians is

Table 3-5
Manpower Programs and Effect on Arrests

	Number of Arrests		Decline (Percent)
	1960-1962	*1964-1966*	
Direct Relocation	51	21	59
Adult Vocational Training	48	30	38

much higher in the non-Indian settlements close to the reservations than in areas far removed from the principal centers of Indian population.[41] For this reason, employment opportunities and advancement are more restricted in the former location.

The 1972 redirection in the employment assistance program has brought about another major change. The new policy is to have clients bring their funds with them to field offices from their home reservations.[c] For example, suppose an Indian wished to take a course in welding under the adult vocational training program. Before 1972 he would have had to apply for services at an urban center which not only offered the course, but also had money available to serve him. Often this method worked acceptably, but always the client's ability to take training depended upon his willingness to go where the money was available, when the money was available. Lack of funds could prevent a client from taking the course he wanted. Moreover, if there were no funds where welding courses were offered, the individual would have to accept his second or third choice of training, or perhaps take no training at all. Placing money at the agency enables the client to determine his training program more closely, because he and his reservation agency control the disbursement of money. If there is money available for training at all, it is made available through offices located on the reservation.[42]

Not only have the direct employment and adult vocational training programs been reoriented to deemphasize urban relocation, but the funding and number of persons served has declined in recent years (table 3-1).

Since 1970-1972 the funding for these programs has decreased and the number of persons served has declined significantly. The budget decline and the redirection of the program has resulted in reductions of 60-90 percent in the staffs in the field office cities.[43] As a result of limited staff it is much more difficult to provide adequate support services to the Indians who do come to the cities for employment and training.

Given the relatively strong evaluation of this program in many of the studies cited previously, one is forced to attribute part of the decline in funding and participants in these programs to a lack of leadership in the central office of the Employment Assistance Division in Washington, D.C. There is no evidence that the Bureau of Indian Affairs has used the past success of these programs as justification for continued expansion in terms of its budget presentations to Congress. The 1978 budget justification estimates contain so little information of an evaluative nature that a legislator would probably become quite frustrated if he tried to base a funding decision on rational considerations.

What is clearly needed at this time is a major evaluation of the employment assistance program. It has been ten years since this was done and even the

---

[c]Of course, he does not physically carry these funds from the agency to the urban job placement center; they are channeled through the financial disbursing channels of the bureau.

previous analysis was undertaken by academics who were quite independent of the BIA. One important part of the evaluation should be to determine whether the programs function more effectively in urban areas as compared to those who receive services on or near reservations.

The need for this evaluation is particularly critical because there is evidence that the efficiency of the program has fallen. To quote from a recent BIA audit report:

"The data we collected shows that about 13 percent of the people who enter the Adult Vocational Training Program end up with jobs related to their training. Although a reliable performance base is not available for comparison purposes, the weight of evidence indicates that the AVT success rate, as measured by job placements, has declined significantly over the last five years. We attribute the decline to a general relaxation of established admission and performance requirements.

. . . One principal criticism of the Direct Employment Assistance Program is that a large share of the money is being used to supplement income instead of helping people find satisfactory employment. Nevertheless the program still works and shows a good success rate even though it is difficult to measure success because of the varied, and often questionable, use of the program."[44]

In addition to relaxed screening, some persons in the field employment offices indicated that the agency sends those least likely to succeed to the city "to get rid of them" and refers the more able for training and employment in the local area. Moreover, a single person participating in the training or direct employment programs in the city receives about $55-$62 a week for living expenses. Many persons cannot make ends meet with this meager income partly because they may be spending 35-40 percent of their income on housing. After a period of time they simply give up and return to the reservation.

Part of the reason that so few persons have been finding training-related employment in recent years is that many are leaving the program before graduation. While two-thirds remained until graduation in the 1960s, only 40-50 percent have been completing training from 1972-1976. Another possible reason for the decline in the percentage in training-related employment is the lack of appropriate jobs on or near the reservation.

As indicated in chapter 1, reservation unemployment has been approximately 40 percent for the past twenty years. An evaluation of the existing programs should consider the fact that some reservations have limited development prospects and that serious thought should be given to continuing and even increasing the number of persons moving from these areas to cities with available jobs.

Department of Labor Programs

Beginning in the late 1960s the Department of Labor began enrolling Indians in the various poverty and manpower programs developed for the general population. In 1970, about 10,000 urban Indians participated with the bulk of participants enrolled in the Neighborhood Youth Corps. Total expenditures on behalf of urban Indians by the Department of Labor in 1970 amounted to approximately $10 million.[45]

In 1973 the United States Congress passed the Comprehensive Employment and Training Act (CETA) which brought a number of discrete and often competing programs together into one overall manpower effort.

Section 302 of Title III requires that special comprehensive employment and training programs be established for Indians regardless of where they reside.[46] This includes such programs as on-the-job training, work experience, skill and classroom training, and public service employment; and such services as child care, transportation, and counseling.

Section 304 of Title III provides for summer youth programs, generally focusing on work experience.

Titles II and VI provide primarily for public service employment programs. Urban Indians are not eligible to participate in the latter.

During 1976 approximately $20 million was spent by the CETA program on urban Indians. The total number of participants was 20,000 with about 7,000 obtaining unsubsidized employment after participating in the CETA program. On a national basis (including urban and nonurban Indians) participants in the program earned $2.11 an hour before participation and $2.81 an hour in unsubsidized employment after participation.[47]

Under Section 302, Title III, public and nonprofit agencies are authorized as prime sponsors and receive the Indian CETA grants. Grants are also let to Indian tribes on federal and state reservations, under Title II and VI and Section 304 of Title III (which is for summer youth programs).

The experience obtained by the CETA program sponsored by the Dallas Inter-Tribal Center is fairly typical. From October 1, 1976 to June 30, 1977 total enrollment was 211 (including 18 carried over from the previous fiscal year). By the end of the period, 138 had left the program including those completing training. Less than half or 62 had obtained jobs. Of the 138 terminations, 55 either quit during training or were involuntarily separated.[48]

The Indian CETA program in Minneapolis operates a day labor program designed to provide emergency or temporary employment for local residents. Any Indian who is on public assistance or who has been unemployed for two weeks or more is eligible.

Each applicant is registered and screened by an employment counselor for specific skills and abilities and is subsequently referred for employment.

The program contracts with employers to meet labor requirements. The program handles all of the payroll functions and covers each employee with workmen's compensation and unemployment insurance. Transportation or bus tokens are provided to get workers to the job site.[49]

It is clear that the Indian CETA program and the Bureau of Indian Affairs' Direct Employment and Adult Institutional Training Programs have overlapping purposes. The BIA trains reservation Indians and finds employment for them in cities or on reservations, but does not provide these services to Indians who have resided for a considerable time in an urban area. The Indian CETA program provides its services for Indians regardless of location and irrespective of whether they have lived in the city for many years. However, the BIA does function as a job referral agency in urban areas and often graduates of the CETA program will go to the BIA to obtain assistance in finding a job.[50]

Day Labor

Daily pay is a major factor in the employment of urban Indians. For example, a 1970 survey of three hundred Indians in Chicago indicated eighty-eight, or 29 percent, earned their living as daily pay workers.[51] Moreover, the proportion of workers engaged in daily pay activities had increased from 1966-1970.

The advantage that the daily pay system holds for many American Indians is that it provides a flexibility that is otherwise unavailable. The individual can go to work in the morning or not depending upon his preference at that time. If he is temporarily incapacitated on Monday morning, he doesn't feel the pressure of having to report for work at eight o'clock. If there is a powwow in Milwaukee or Minneapolis, he is free to take off and attend without having to notify his employer. The flexibility that employment through daily pay offices provides is the most important factor in the reliance of many American Indians on this form of job activity.[52]

A disadvantage is that the wage rate is below what the individual would make if he obtained a permanent job. The difference in wage rates paid to daily pay workers and permanent employees is taken by the daily pay office. In addition, the $18 or $20 that a daily pay worker earns each day all too frequently disappears for one or another immediate expense; the pay check is not a lump sum from which rent, for example, can be deducted. This means there is often difficulty for daily pay workers in meeting rent, utility, and emergency bills. This would be less likely to occur if the same amount of money were available in a lump sum twice a month. However, daily pay workers indicate that a major problem in regard to obtaining full-time employment is having enough money to get along until the first pay check is received.

Job Discrimination—A Case Study of Seattle

That urban Indians are victims of social and economic discrimination is a statement that meets with general acceptance among interested academics and certainly within the native American community. However, little systematic research regarding the dimensions and intensity of this discrimination has been undertaken.

An extensive survey of discrimination was carried out by Bahr, Chadwick, and Strauss in Seattle. At the time of the study the unemployment rate for Indians was 20 percent for females and 38 percent for males.[53] Many of the Seattle Indians surveyed reported experiencing racial discrimination in employment. The discrimination reported occurred with respect to both job finding and advancement. One-fifth of the Indian respondents claimed that they had been refused jobs solely because they were Indian. Table 3-6 indicates the results of the survey.

Two-thirds of the Indians are convinced that employers in Seattle treat them unfairly, and one-half feel that they would have an easier time finding work if they were not Indian. These perceptions of employment discrimination are not simply the consequences of oversensitive Indians placing racial interpretations on unsuccessful attempts to obtain work in a city with a depressed economy.[54] A substantial number of whites agreed that Indians face discriminatory barriers to jobs in Seattle.

Summary

From the early 1950s until 1972, the Bureau of Indian Affairs operated a major training and relocation program. Reservation Indians were placed in positions in major metropolitan areas. Since 1972 the program has undergone a change in policy. Most participants are trained and find jobs near the reservations; fewer are being sent to the cities.

According to the various evaluative criteria employed, the Bureau of Indian

Table 3-6
Perceptions of Anti-Indian Employment Discrimination

	Indians			Whites		
	Agree	Uncertain	Disagree	Agree	Uncertain	Disagree
Indians have a harder time than whites getting a job in Seattle	81	8	11	63	18	18
Employers in this city tend to treat Indians unfairly	64	14	22	40	35	25
If I were not an Indian I would have an easier time finding a job	48	11	42	–	–	–

Source: Howard M. Bahr, Bruce A. Chadwick, and Joseph Strauss, "Discrimination Against Urban Indians in Seattle," *The Indian Historian* 5 (1972), p. 6. Reprinted with permission.

Affairs' manpower and training programs were reasonably successful. However, in recent years their efficiency and effectiveness has declined. One reason for this is a relaxation of admission standards for the program.

The Department of Labor operates the CETA program on behalf of reservation and urban Indians. Some aspects of this program duplicate the manpower programs undertaken by the Bureau of Indian Affairs.

The tendency of many urban Indians to prefer daily pay jobs is widespread. Although day work allows the person flexibility in terms of the allocation of his time, the rate of pay is less than a permanent employee could obtain for doing similar work. In addition, there is no chance for advancement.

Anecdotal evidence indicates widespread employment discrimination against urban Indians. However, despite the importance of this problem almost no research has been done to describe the extent or dimensions of this discrimination.

Notes

1. *International Labour Review* 51 (June 1945):781-782. Also, it was estimated in 1944 that 14,059 Indians could have been recruited and placed in off-reservation employment if more intensive recruitment and placement services had been instituted and if transportation had been made more readily available.

2. U.S. Department of Interior, Bureau of Indian Affairs, "The Bureau of Indian Affairs' Voluntary Employment Assistance Services Program" (Washington, D.C.: Bureau of Indian Affairs, no date), mimeographed, p. 2.

3. U.S. Congress, House Committee on Interior and Insular Affairs, "Survey Report on the Bureau of Indian Affairs" (Washington, D.C.: U.S. Government Printing Office, 1954), p. 23.

4. U.S. Department of Interior, Bureau of Indian Affairs, "Policies and Programs of the Bureau of Indian Affairs" (Washington, D.C., no date), unpublished.

5. U.S. Department of Interior, Bureau of Indian Affairs, "Employment Assistance Programs" (Washington, D.C., 1972), unpublished.

6. U.S. Department of Interior, Bureau of Indian Affairs, Branch of Employment Assistance, "Adult Vocational Training Services: Questions and Answers" (Washington, D.C.: Bureau of Indian Affairs, no date), mimeographed, pp. 1-3.

7. Lawrence Clinton, Bruce A. Chadwick, and Howard M. Bahr, "Urban Relocation Reconsidered: Antecedents of Employment Among Indian Males," *Rural Sociology* 40, no. 2 (Summer 1975):124-125.

8. Theodore D. Graves and Charles A. Lave, "Determinants of Urban Migrant Indian Wages," *Human Organization*, 31 (Spring 1972):47.

9. Harry Martin, "Correlates of Adjustment Among Urban Indians in an

Urban Environment," *Human Organization* 23 (Winter 1964):290-295; Murray Wax and Rosalie Wax, "The Enemies of the People," in Howard S. Becker, ed., *Institutions and the Person* (Chicago: Aldine Publishing Co., 1968).

10. Bruce A. Chadwick and Lynn C. White, "Correlates of Length of Urban Residence Among the Spokane Indians," *Human Organization* 32 (Spring 1973):9-16; Martin, "Correlates of Adjustment Among Urban Indians," pp. 292-293.

11. Robert S. Weppner, "Urban Economic Opportunities: The Example of Denver," in Jack O. Waddell and O. Michael Watson, eds., *The American Indian in Urban Society* (Boston: Little, Brown and Co., 1971), pp. 245-273.

12. Graves and Lave, "Determinants of Urban Migrant Indian Wages," pp. 47-61.

13. Theodore D. Graves, "The Personal Adjustment of Navajo Indian Migrants to Denver, Colorado," *American Anthropologist* 72 (February 1970):135-154.

14. Martin, "Correlates of Adjustment Among Urban Indians," pp. 293-294.

15. Graves, "Personal Adjustment of Navajo Indian Migrants," p. 42.

16. Graves and Lave, "Determinants of Urban Migrant Indian Wages," p. 52; Peter Snyder, "The Social Environment of the Urban Indian," in Waddell and Watson, eds., *American Indian in Urban Society*, pp. 207-243; Clinton, Chadwick, and Bahr, "Urban Relocation Reconsidered," p. 125.

17. Graves, "Personal Adjustment of Navajo Indian Migrants," pp. 41-46; Graves and Lave, "Determinants of Urban Migrant Indian Wages," pp. 50-56; and Clinton, Chadwick, and Bahr, "Urban Relocation Reconsidered," pp. 125-126.

18. Clinton, Chadwick, and Bahr, "Urban Relocation Reconsidered," pp. 128-129.

19. Lawrence Clinton, Bruce A. Chadwick, and Howard M. Bahr, "Vocational Training for Indian Migrants: Correlates of 'Success' in a Federal Program," *Human Organization* 32, no. 1 (Spring 1973):17.

20. Sar A. Levitan, *Anti-Poverty Work and Training Efforts: Goals and Reality* (Washington, D.C.: National Manpower Policy Task Force, 1967); Sar A. Levitan and G.L. Mangum, *Federal Training and Work Programs in the Sixties* (Ann Arbor: Institute of Labor and Industrial Relations, 1969); U.S. Department of Labor, *Manpower Report of the President, 1971* (Washington, D.C.: U.S. Government Printing Office, 1972), p. 53.

21. U.S. Department of Interior, Bureau of Indian Affairs, "A Follow-Up Study of 1963 Recipients of the Employment Assistance Program" (Washington, D.C.: Bureau of Indian Affairs, October 1966), mimeographed, p. 43; revised (July 1968), mimeographed, p. 26.

22. H.H. London, *How Fare MDTA Ex-Trainees: An Eighteen Months Follow-Up Study of Five Hundred Such Persons* (Columbia: University of Missouri, 1967), mimeographed.

23. Clinton, Chadwick, and Bahr, "Vocational Training," p. 20.

24. U.S. Congress, *Indian Relocation and Industrial Development Programs*, Report of a Special Subcommittee on Interior and Insular Affairs, 85th Congress, First Session (1958), p. 3.

25. Harry W. Martin, Robert L. Leon, and John Gladfelter, "The Salt River Reservation: A Proposal for the Development of Its Human and Natural Resources" (a consultation report to the Bureau of Indian Affairs, 1967), mimeographed, p. 11.

26. Alan Sorkin, *American Indians and Federal Aid* (Washington, D.C.: The Brookings Institution, 1971), p. 123.

27. Paul Brinker and Benjamin Taylor, "Southern Plains Indian Relocation Returnees," *Human Organization* 33, no. 1 (Spring 1974):141.

28. Weppner, "Urban Economic Opportunities," p. 254.

29. Brinker and Taylor, "Southern Plains Indian," p. 144.

30. P. Collier, "The Red Man's Burden," *Ramparts* 8:26-38.

31. Brinker and Taylor, "Southern Plains Indian," p. 143.

32. Weppner, "Urban Economic Opportunities," pp. 254-268.

33. Robert M. Cullum, "Assisted Navajo Relocation, 1952-1956" (Washington, D.C.: Bureau of Indian Affairs, Gallup Area Office, 1957), mimeographed, p. 8, as cited in Peter P. Dorner, "The Economic Position of the American Indians: Their Resources and Potential for Development" (Ph.D. dissertation, Harvard University, 1959), p. 191.

34. Chadwick and White, "Correlates of Length of Urban Residence," pp. 9-15.

35. Theodore D. Graves and Minor Van Arsdale, "Values, Expectations, and Relocation: The Navajo Migrant to Denver," *Human Organization* 25 (1966):307.

36. Chadwick and White, "Correlates of Length of Urban Residence," p. 15.

37. Theodore D. Graves, "Alternative Models for the Study of Urban Migration," *Human Organization* 25 (Winter 1966):299.

38. U.S. Department of Interior, Bureau of Indian Affairs, "A Follow-Up Study of 1963 Recipients," pp. 21, 34, and 47. No distinction was made between misdemeanors and felonies.

39. Nationally, drunkenness alone accounts for 71 percent of all Indian arrests. See Omer Stuart, "Questions Regarding American Indian Criminality," *Human Organization* 23 (Spring 1964):61.

40. U.S. Department of Interior, Bureau of Indian Affairs, "Annual Statistical Summary, 1971" (Washington, D.C., 1972), mimeographed; unpublished tabulation provided by Mr. Robert Delaware, Branch of Employment Assistance (Summer 1976).

41. R.A. Leuffen, "Prejudice and Discrimination Against Navajos in a Mining Community," *The Kiva* 30 (1964):1-17; A.L. Wahrhaftig and R.K.

Thomas, "Renaissance and Repression: The Oklahoma Cherokee," *Transaction* (February 1969):22.

42. U.S. Department of Interior, Bureau of Indian Affairs, Division of Employment Assistance, "New Directions—Ideas Behind the Working Concepts of the Redirected Employment Assistance Program" (Washington, D.C., June 1972), unpublished.

43. Interviews with employment assistance personnel, Chicago, Los Angeles, and Dallas (August 1977).

44. U.S. Department of Interior, Bureau of Indian Affairs, Director of Audit and Investigation, "Review of Adult Vocational Training and Direct Employment Assistance Programs" (memorandum to commissioner, May 11, 1976), p. 1.

45. Sar A. Levitan and Barbara Hetrick, *Big Brothers' Indian Programs: With Reservations* (New York: McGraw-Hill Book Co., 1971), p. 182.

46. U.S. Department of Labor, Employment and Training Administration, *Indian and Native American Programs, Fiscal Year 1976 Report* (Washington, D.C.: U.S. Department of Labor, 1976), p. 7.

47. Ibid., pp. 18, 21, and 23.

48. Dallas Inter-Tribal Center, "CETA Program Status Summary" (October 1, 1976 to June 30, 1977), unpublished tabulation. In 1975 over 80 percent of those Indians participating in the Bureau of Indian Affairs' Adult Vocational Training Program in Dallas found jobs upon completion of training.

49. Minneapolis Regional Native American Center, "Day Labor Division" (no date), printed brochure.

50. Interview with Mr. Al Lerner, Los Angeles Field Employment Assistance Office, Bureau of Indian Affairs (August 1977).

51. John K. White, "Patterns in American Indian Employment: A Study of the Work Habits of American Indians in Chicago, Illinois" (Chicago: St. Augustine's Indian Center, 1971), p. 9.

52. Ibid., p. 6.

53. Howard M. Bahr, Bruce A. Chadwick, and Joseph Strauss, "Discrimination Against Urban Indians in Seattle," *The Indian Historian* 5 (1972):5.

54. Ibid., p. 6.

4 Indian Health and Alcoholism

The Indian Health Service (IHS), which has had the responsibility for providing health care to American Indians since 1955, has generally restricted services to those native Americans living on federally recognized reservations.[1]

This agency provides comprehensive free medical care to reservation Indians regardless of income. However, if an Indian leaves the reservation and moves to an urban location, he is usually unable to receive medical care from the Indian Health Service. Many urban Indians are medically indigent and do not avail themselves of urban health facilities intended for the general population. This has served to create a serious health problem among urban Indians and has resulted in a significantly lower standard of health than that prevailing among the non-Indian urban population. Thus, many urban Indians receive only limited medical assistance or fail to obtain any health services; others appear at hospitals as emergency cases; and some have to make costly and time consuming trips back to their home reservation or community to utilize the free health services provided by the IHS.[2]

Generally, new Indian arrivals to urban areas are unfamiliar with existing health facilities and are uncertain as to whether they are eligible to utilize such health institutions. These individuals are often reluctant to go to local hospitals because they lack the funds to pay for care, preferring to wait until they have the money to finance a trip to an Indian health facility. By delaying treatment they risk more serious illness. In addition, Indians may be reluctant to use existing facilities in cities because of language problems, or due to ignorance concerning which services are available.[3]

Health care facilities in urban areas, both city, state, and county, have not worked with federal health service agencies to assure general cooperation in the provision of services, and particularly in identifying and meeting urban Indian health needs. Moreover, these organizations have not even begun to prepare a comprehensive approach to meeting these problems.

Urban Indian Health Care Programs

Initially Indian and other community leaders established small voluntary clinics which operated on a part-time basis and charged no fee for services rendered. Local doctors, dentists, and nurses donated their time and various organizations gave used laboratory and medical equipment to the clinics. Shortly after these

47

institutions began operating, large numbers of Indian patients were being treated at these urban Indian health facilities. This led to a greater understanding of the actual medical needs of the community. As these voluntary free clinics expanded, it became most important to obtain sufficient funding to care for the increasing patient load. Although most of these health facilities had relied on private donations in their early stages of development, Title V of the Indian Health Care Improvement Act of 1976 provides limited federal funding for urban Indian health programs.

The purpose of Title V is to encourage the establishment of programs in urban areas which make health services more accessible to the Indian population. The Indian Health Service is authorized to enter into contracts with urban Indian groups to establish outreach and referral services, in addition to direct health care programs for urban Indians.

The legislation authorizes $5 million for urban Indian health programs in 1978; $10 million in 1979; and $15 million in 1980.[4] During 1976 approximately $3 million was spent for urban Indian health care (see table 4-1).

Federal funding has enabled many of the health projects to generate considerable additional financial support. For example, the total budget of the Milwaukee Health Center is $750,000 but only $150,000 is obtained from the federal government.[5]

Table 4-1
Funding Levels—Urban Indian Health Projects, 1976

City	Amount
Chicago	$ 50,000
Dallas	150,000
Denver	85,000
Detroit	68,000
Green Bay	50,000
Milwaukee	150,000
Minneapolis	275,000
Oklahoma City	180,000
Omaha	50,000
Portland	100,000
Seattle	612,000
Spokane	70,000
Tulsa	75,000
Wichita	80,000
Montana (state wide)	100,000
California (state wide)	807,000

Source: Unpublished data provided by the U.S. Public Health Service, June 1977.

The level of federal support for urban Indian health programs is very inadequate. The Indian Health Service spends $420 million a year for health programs serving reservation Indians.[6] Since about one-half of all Indians presently live in cities, an appropriation of $3 million for urban Indian health is less than 1 percent the level of appropriation for reservation Indians. Although it is true that urban Indians have alternative sources of health care and reservation Indians frequently do not, the degree of disparity in federal funding between reservation and urban Indians is indefensible.

Health Status of Urban Indians

There is a serious lack of information regarding the health status of urban Indians. This is in sharp contrast to the considerable statistics maintained by the IHS regarding mortality and morbidity among reservation Indians.[7] The data presented here regarding urban Indian health status are fragmentary and incomplete, but they are the only information available.

The much higher number of hospital days per thousand population experienced by the community served through the Seattle Indian Health Board in comparison to other groups is clear (see table 4-2). This occurs because of the Indians' poor health status, limited economic circumstances and particular health problems such as alcoholism. Only 5 percent of the Seattle Indian Health Board patients surveyed had health insurance, 55 percent of the patients were transients (moving back and forth from the reservation to the city), and 60 percent of the patients had low incomes.[8]

The persons using the Seattle Medical Clinic indicated the same general disease pattern as that found among reservation Indians in the Northwest. Morbidity rates from infectious diseases, particularly those affecting ears and the

Table 4-2
Comparative Hospital Utilization Statistics, Seattle Indian Health Board

Hospital Inpatient	Under Age 65, Short-Term Nonmaternity Days Per 1,000 Population
Seattle Indian population	944
U.S. population	835
State of Washington population	519
Group health-Puget Soung (approximate)	400
Typical insured plan	777
Typical well managed, closed panel HMO	450-600

Source: Indian Health Task Force Six, *Final Report to the American Indian Policy Review Commission* (Washington, D.C.: U.S. Government Printing Office, 1976), p. 149.

upper respiratory tract were high. Alcohol abuse and injuries were common medical problems (see table 4-3). In addition, stress, perhaps caused by the problems associated with urban adjustment, is reflected in the incidence of mild to severe emotional disturbance. Only one chronic disease, diabetes, is highly prevalent in the Seattle Clinic patients; its incidence being more than twice that of the general population.

Morbidity data obtained by the American Indian Health Service of Chicago, Inc., indicated the following health problems were most common: gastrointestinal diseases (gastritis, enteritis, pancreatitis); neuro-psychiatric illness; respiratory diseases such as tuberculosis, bronchitis, and pneumonia; diabetes and obesity; and otitis media.[9] Of the fifteen hundred persons using the Chicago health facility, less than 10 percent either had insurance or were able to pay for health services from their own resources.[10]

In the Minneapolis metropolitan area, the infant death rate among Indians is

Table 4-3

Frequency Distribution of the Most Common Conditions of Seattle Indian Health Board Medical Clinic Patients May-September 1973

Condition	Number	Rate per 100
Otitis media	196	9.1
Alcohol abuse and/or dependency	123	6.6
Lacerations, contusions, abrasions	119	6.4
Febrile URI (influenza-like)	98	5.3
Vaginitis	89	4.8
Common cold	85	4.6
Atopic dermatitis	71	3.8
Pharyngitis	70	3.8
Benign hypertension	68	3.6
Diabetes	67	3.6
Pregnancy	54	2.9
Anxiety with symptoms	49	2.6
Depression	46	2.5
Localized skin infections	45	2.4
Sprains, strains	43	2.3
Obesity	42	2.3
Iron deficiency anemia	39	2.1
Anxiety	39	2.1
Acute bronchitis	34	1.8
Pharyngitis strep	31	1.7

Source: Indian Health Task Force Six, *Final Report to the American Indian Policy Review Commission* (Washington, D.C.: U.S. Government Printing Office, 1976), p. 149.

more than 50 percent higher than among non-Indians. The annual infant death rate in Minneapolis for all races during 1968-1970 was 22.9 infant deaths per 1,000 live births; in Hennepin County for the same years the Indian infant death rate was 35.3 infant deaths per 1,000 live births. Ramsey County (St. Paul) had an Indian infant death rate of 31.0 percent per 1,000 live births for the same years.[11] Moreover, the infant death rate among Indians living on reservations in Minnesota is about one-half the infant death rate among Indians living in urban areas.[12]

A major factor in the high infant death rate is that Indian mothers do not receive prenatal care as early in pregnancy as white mothers. In 1969, 62.4 percent of white mothers in Minnesota received prenatal care during the first three months of pregnancy and only 0.7 percent received no care at any time during their pregnancy. However, in the Minneapolis metropolitan region, from 1967 through 1970 only 29.7 percent of Indian mothers began prenatal care in the first three months of their pregnancy, and 8.4 percent received no prenatal care at all.[13]

In the Uptown section of Chicago many Indian women do not take advantage of available prenatal medical facilities until the third trimester of pregnancy. Many of the expectant mothers are undernourished and have a low hemoglobin count; their newborn babies are highly susceptible to infectious diseases. These women consider childbearing a natural life experience and a very personal matter. This attitude and feelings of modesty preclude many Indian women from seeking prenatal and even postnatal care.[14]

Beginning in August 1972, the Indian Health Board of Minneapolis initiated a survey of all known Indian households in the city. By January 1973, 389 households had been visited. Despite the fact that nearly 70 percent of the households had some form of health coverage, the interviewers found only 8.2 percent obtained care from private physicians and dentists.

Interviewers found numerous health problems in the households that they surveyed (see table 4-4). In 11.6 percent of the households there was a person requiring immediate inpatient hospital care.[15]

A second household survey of health problems in Minneapolis, undertaken in 1974, found the following:[16]

1. Nearly 400 persons had chronic diseases of whom 62 were not receiving any medical treatment;
2. Seventy-three persons had mental or emotional problems of which 45 were receiving assistance;
3. Within the past year, 128 injuries had occurred which were serious enough to require a doctor's care, but 35 were not treated; and
4. Forty-three percent of households reported transportation problems in getting to a doctor or clinic.

Table 4-4

Health Problems Found in Interview Survey of 389 Minneapolis Households

	Households	
Type of Problem	Number	Percent
Dental problem	134	34
Eye or vision problem	54	14
Hearing problem	22	6
Preventive or diagnostic concerns	94	24
Mental health problem	25	6
Alcohol or drug problem	37	10
Chronic disease and disability	44	11
Acute medical problems	84	21
Other problems	3	10
No medical or dental problems	44	11

Source: Charles McCreary, Charles Deegan, Jr., and David Thompson, "Indian Health in Minnesota," *Minnesota Medicine* 56, no. 2 (October 1973): 89. Reprinted with permission.

Note: More than one problem was found in many households.

At the same time that medical survey was undertaken, a dental survey was carried out at the clinic. The major findings were:

1. One in five of those seeking help required immediate emergency attention;
2. An average of one prosthetic device (bridge, partial or full denture) was needed for each person 15 years of age or more; and
3. Ninety-one percent of those over 14 had periodontal disease.

The large number of urban Indians with dental disease indicates severe underutilization of existing dental facilities. This problem seems to be widespread. For example, a survey undertaken in Dallas, Texas, indicates that 40 percent of the native Americans residing there have never had any dental care while in Dallas.[17] Similar findings were reported in a Minneapolis survey.[18]

In Minnesota accidents are the leading cause of death among Indians. Because the life expectancy of Minnesota Indians is less than for all races, the Indian is far less likely to die of the diseases of aging than are non-Indians (see table 4-5).

A health and mobility survey was recently completed on five Indian reservations in Minnesota (Red Lake, White Earth, Leech Lake, Mille Lacs, and Upper Sioux). One-third of all the households surveyed included at least one person who had lived in an urban area. Regarding the latter, 55 percent reported problems in obtaining health care in the city. Moreover, one major reason why half of the former city dwellers returned to the reservation was to obtain health

Table 4-5
Leading Causes of Death of Indians and for All Races in Minnesota
(in percent)

Cause of Death	Indian 1968-1970	All Races 1970
Accidents	23.2	6.3
Heart disease	19.7	37.6
Cancer	7.9	18.1
Cerebrovascular disease	7.9	12.7
Influenza and pneumonia	5.8	3.2
Cirrhosis	5.4	1.1
Early infancy	5.2	2.2
Diabetes mellitus	4.6	1.8
Other causes	21.0	17.0

Source: Chalres McCreary, Charles Deegan, Jr., and David Thompson, "Indian Health in Minnesota," *Minnesota Medicine* 56, no. 2 (October 1973): 88-89. Reprinted with permission.
Note: About three-fifths of all Indians in Minnesota are urban Indians.

care, which is readily accessible and free of charge.[19] It is a gross injustice to virtually force native Americans to return to the reservations for treatment of physical illness.

Traditional Medicine

Although the above surveys indicate that urban Indians have many unmet health needs, and frequently do not visit physicians when medically appropriate, this does not indicate that these persons are receiving no health or medical care. A study carried out under the auspices of the Urban Indian Health Board of San Francisco found that 28 percent of the families surveyed reported using some form of traditional Indian medicine during the five years preceding the interview. Indians from the Southwest were most likely to use traditional medicine. Moreover, many who were well educated, had high incomes, and were well established in the city, continued to use traditional Indian medicine. Such factors as ability to use a native language, degree to which friendships are restricted to Indians, and preference for living on the reservation are positively related to the use of traditional medicine.[20]

The data also support the contention that the demand for traditional medicine is an important reason why Indians return to the reservation. Moreover, most of those who did this utilized scientific medicine as well as traditional medicine. Hence, a double purpose trip to receive both scientific and native medicine was an important reason for returning to the reservation.

One of the greatest needs in the urban Indian community is for an intensive effort in certain areas of preventive medicine and chronic disease care including the following:[21]

1. Audiology testing and ear checks of preschool children;
2. Vision testing of preschool children, as well as tonometry in adults and routine funduscopic exams in people with diabetes mellitus;
3. Family counseling on methods of birth control;
4. Routine screening for venereal disease;
5. Routine evaluation for tuberculosis; and
6. Medical control of obesity, diabetes, mellitus, and asthma.

However, most urban Indian health centers are overwhelmed by the number of patients who utilize their faciliites for curative medical care. There is too little staff and equipment to enable these facilities to undertake much preventive care at present levels of funding.

Most urban Indian health centers do not charge for the bulk of their services. Some relate charges for ancillary services such as x-ray and laboratory tests to the person's income, but because of the low economic status of most of their patients, few pay more than a nominal charge.

One exception to this policy occurs at the Indian Health Board of Minneapolis, a facility with three doctors and two dentists, that averages eight thousand patients a year. It is estimated that one-half the Indians in Minneapolis use this facility. The clinic policy is to charge for its services with fees and other expenses not scaled to income. It is felt that Indian people must be educated regarding the importance of paying for health care as part of one's regular budget.[22]

Depending on the city, about 20-40 percent of the Indian population can be described as being in a transient status. Most of these persons are moving back and forth from the reservation. If they require long-term care, there will be discontinuities in treatment partly because their medical records will have to be sent from the Indian Health Service on the reservation to the city and vice versa. This does occur but with attendant delays.

One of the greatest needs within the clinics is a mental health program. As indicated in the morbidity data described earlier, anxiety and depression as well as other mental and emotional problems are extensive among urban Indians. However, at present it is only possible to refer persons to psychologists and psychiatrists employed by public agencies. Because these organizations serve the general population, Indians are reluctant to use their services. However, at present levels of funding, it is not possible for most urban Indian clinics to provide mental health services.

The Dallas Free Clinic—A Case Study

In Dallas a free walk-in clinic has been the Dallas Inter-Tribal Center's most useful program in terms of community participation. Patients feel comfortable at the clinic because it is an important part of their center.

As of April 1, 1977, thirty-four hundred patients representing fifty-six tribes had registered with the medical clinic since its opening in 1971. Primary health care services are offered at no cost to patients two evenings per week.[23] (Community surveys conducted prior to the opening of the clinic indicated evening hours were most convenient for the patients.) The clinic has no age, income, or residency restrictions on patients. They are required, however, to be at least one-quarter Indian blood.

The clinic is staffed completely by volunteer doctors, nurses, and laboratory technicians from the Dallas area. Regular employees include an Indian receptionist and Indian outreach workers. Plans are being formulated for training Indian nurses' aides. The clinic has a community-based board of directors and an advisory board comprised of physicians and other professionals which serve in a consultant capacity.

Funding is obtained from occasional small private donations that provide for only a minimal amount of the needed medicines and equipment. Clinic facilities include four examination rooms, a laboratory, a medicine room, a waiting room, and office space.

Despite having to operate with inadequate funding and a completely volunteer medical staff, the clinic has established a strong rapport with the Indian community. Currently the medical staff sees about sixty patients during the two clinic sessions per week, with an average of twelve new patients registering weekly.

The clinic maintains a system of follow-up for patients referred elsewhere. Approximately one thousand have been referred to other agencies since the clinic opened. However, a survey has shown that only one-half of these patients actually obtain needed services.[24]

The professional staff indicate that clinic hours need to be increased to accommodate the growing Indian population in Dallas. (It is estimated that the present Indian population in Dallas will double in five years.) Dental, family planning, and maternal and child health programs need to be added to the services offered. A nurse practitioner or physician's assistant should be employed to head the clinic staff. Other salaried staff positions required include a nurse's aide, a laboratory technician, and a pediatric nurse. The additional staff would enable the clinic to extend its hours to at least twenty per week.

Lack of adequate funding is the only serious obstacle limiting the clinic's present and future health care delivery system to the city's Indians.

Alcoholism

Alcoholism with its attendant social, physical, and psychological consequences is one of the primary health problems among American Indians. The Indian death rate from cirrhosis of the liver is approximately three times that in the total U.S. population.[25] Alcohol-related arrests are greater and alcohol-related traffic fatalities are also much higher for Indians in comparison to non-Indians. In addition, the high suicide rate among some Indian groups appears to be directly related to high levels of alcohol consumption.

The Indian Health Service Task Force on Alcoholism concluded that:

although it is unsafe to generalize, what few studies that have been done on drinking patterns in Indians have a certain consistency. Drinking is widespread, reaching its peak of frequency in the age groups 25-44. Males usually outnumber females by a ratio of at least 3 to 1. By the age of 15 most youth of both sexes have tried alcohol and some are drinking regularly. After the age of 40, there is a noticeable decline in the number of drinkers and the extent of drinking. Many Indians of all ages are total abstainers.[26]

In Minnesota where the total Indian population is 35,000, 40 percent or 14,000 people have a serious alcohol problem. Moreover, there are 8,750 Indian youth from ages 11 to 18 years old using abusive chemicals or drugs. Glue sniffing is on the increase and now comprises 73 percent of all offenses for American Indian youth in Minnesota as compared to 15 percent for non-Indian youth.[27]

It is estimated that in Boston, which has an Indian population of approximately 3,500, there are from 400 to 800 people suffering from alcoholism. Moreover, about 90 percent of the court cases involving native Americans are alcohol related.

In Salt Lake City, Utah, where Indians comprise one-third of 1 percent of the population, about 40 percent of persons arrested for public intoxication are Indians. Considering alcohol-related crimes (driving under the influence, liquor law violations, and drunkenness) in 1975, Indians comprised 21,069 of the urban arrests, and 2,131 of the rural within the state of Utah.

In Baltimore, approximately 15 percent of the Indian population are considered alocholics. This compares to 5 percent of the non-Indian population in Maryland.[28]

In 1971, reports on urban arrests nationally indicate that 75 percent of all arrests among Indians were alcohol related compared to 33 percent of all arrests for non–Indians. Thus, the Indian/non–Indian alcohol-related urban arrest ratio is 2.27:1.

For juveniles, eighteen years and younger, city arrest data for 1971 indicate that Indians account for 25.1 percent of all arrests which are alochol related in comparison to 7.2 percent for non-Indians.[29]

The Nature of Indian Drinking Problems

Various attempts have been made to discover the causes of American Indian alcoholism and to find effective methods for treatment, rehabilitation, and prevention. Because of individual differences in tribal background, intrafamiliar relationships, and in the degree of acculturation to the city, it is difficult to clearly analyze the problem of urban Indian alcoholism in terms of a useful and basic framework.

Ferguson discusses some of the probable reasons for alcohol abuse among American Indians.[30] Excessive drinking may:

1. Relieve psychological and social stress caused by the pressures for acculturation;
2. Facilitate the release of repressed hostility and aggression;
3. Help attain a state of harmony with nature; or
4. Make for more pleasant social interaction with friends.

Whatever the cause of Indian drinking problems in cities, there appears to be general agreement that (1) few social stigma or moralistic attitudes are associated with Indian alcoholism;[31] (2) there is no evidence of any unusual physiological sensitivity toward alcoholism on the part of any ethnic group, including American Indians;[32] and (3) most Indians drink in groups and solitary drinkers are rare, except for those persons experiencing serious difficulty adjusting to the city.

For many Indian problem drinkers the use of alcohol seems to be their means of dealing with anger and frustration. Drunkenness releases and sometimes redirects pent-up anger. In some cases the anger is associated with frustration resulting from a perceived lack of accomplishment. The latter is related to problems of unemployment and dependence on welfare. Thus, the person without a job has little opportunity to prove himself.[33]

Clinical evidence from St. Augustine's Indian Center in Chicago, which operates an alcoholism treatment program, indicates that excessive drinking does serve as outlet for aggression. Counselors feel that psychodynamic factors are important and that ego-alien behavior occurs when one is under the influence of alcohol. Many of the cases at the center seem to follow Zwerling's and Rosenbaum's description of the etiology of alcoholism, that is, an early disruption of the mother-child relationship, frustrations, rage, ambivalent dependency relationships, and depression.[34]

The impact of culture conflict has long been considered a major cause of Indian alcoholism. Whether acculturation can occur without causing personal conflict and anxiety appears unlikely. For example, Alfred found a significant increase in blood pressure among Navajos after they had moved to Denver, and he concludes that "migration is a source of stress for the Navajos."[35] Half of them returned to the reservation after six months.

The inability of many native Americans to adjust to the demands and pace of urban industrial society (even where the stay in the city is brief as in the case of Eskimos brought to Chicago by the BIA for training) leads to increased anxiety, withdrawal, and alcoholism. A Chicago minister whose congregation included several Eskimo families indicated that occasionally he conducted worship services in their homes because many of the Eskimos were afraid to walk or travel the one mile distance to the church. Such distances surely were no obstacle when the Eskimos were in Alaska. Except for some of the younger, single men, who had been in military service, Eskimos were not used to urban transportation, shopping in supermarkets, and other city amenities.[36]

Heath suggests that according to anthropological studies "the act of drinking, like eating, may in itself have a peculiar significance as a means of expressing corporate solidarity."[37] Recent emphasis on alcohol as a way of expressing group togetherness has been made by Field, Lemert, and Simmons.[38] Whether an Indian is on a reservation or in an urban area he is unlikely to drink alone for long. The pressure to drink with friends is very great. Refusing to accept a drink from another Indian or to buy him one is considered insulting. Unlike other alcoholics, these drinkers are not alienated from their people.

It is surprising how little empirical research has focused on urban Indian alcoholism. The most comprehensive and sophisticated study was done by Graves focusing on Navajo migrants to Denver. Police records of virtually all Navajo males in that city were collected.[39] Since 95 percent of all Indian arrests in Denver were for alcohol-related problems,[40] the arrest rate was used as a proxy to indicate difficulties with drinking.

Graves found that those earning less in Denver than on the reservation had an arrest rate which was more than double those whose earnings in Denver were equal to or exceeded reservation earnings.[41] Those Indians earning less in the city than on the reservation appeared to have reacted to this disappointment and frustration by engaging in heavy drinking.

Earlier it was indicated that peer pressure toward drinking is frequently strong among Indians. Graves found that those Navajos with exclusively Navajo friends had an arrest rate nearly double those with some non-Navajo friends.

Finally, it was found that those migrants whose personal goal structure was unrealistic in view of urban opportunities, experienced the greatest conflict about remaining in the city and drank the heaviest. Thus, those Navajos who subscribed to traditional Navajo values and were rated low in terms of economic values had an arrest rate nearly double those who did not subscribe to traditional values and had high economic values.[42]

Although the problem of alcoholism among native Americans has existed for a long time, it has only been fairly recently that any significant federal effort has been mounted to deal with this problem. The first apparent recognition of alcoholism as a high priority health problem came in October 1968, when the Indian Health Service appointed a task force to review the extent of alcoholism on Indian reservations and communities, evaluate existing programs and re-sources, and provide guidelines and plans of action to assist in meeting the problem. In its report (1970), IHS states that "It is the policy of the Indian Health Service that services and programs for the prevention and comprehensive treatment of alcoholism be given the highest possible priority at all levels of administration."[43]

In 1970, the president's message on the status of American Indians further emphasized the need for program efforts. Funds from the Office of Economic Opportunity (OEO) ($1.2 million) and the National Institute of Mental Health (NIMH) ($750,000) were allocated to IHS to establish thirty-nine Indian projects.[44] Subsequently, the National Institute on Alcohol Abuse and Alcohol-ism was established and became the only federal agency funding Indian alcoholism programs from 1970-1976. In July 1976 the funding authority of the NIAAA was extended for three years. However, the legislation does not specifically authorize funds for Indian projects; in fact, the law as renewed, does not guarantee that projects will be funded. As succinctly stated in the Report of the Committee on Interior and Insular Affairs, United States Senate on the Indian Health Care Improvement Act:

The decision to allocate a portion of NIAAA's funds for Indian programs and to establish an Indian desk within NIAAA to assist in the administration of these programs was purely discretionary, and therefore neither constitutes a guarantee that alcoholism monies will be available for Indians, nor indicates that the federal government has any responsibility to provide alcoholism programs for Indians.[45]

The alcoholism grants, which are administered through the Special Projects Branch, are considered as "demonstration" or start-up grants. Funds are disbursed for a period of 3-6 years. During 1976, 153 Indian alcoholism projects were funded in both urban and rural areas at a cost of $18 million. One-third of these projects were in urban areas.[46] See table 4-6 for a listing of selected projects and their level of funding.

Recent legislation provides for the IHS to take over all the NIAAA programs in Indian alcoholism. This will occur between 1978 and 1982. Perhaps the IHS will place greater emphasis on evaluation than the NIAAA has done so that the most effective methods of dealing with the problem of Indian alcoholism can be developed.

In addition to funding programs to provide direct services to Indian alcoholics, the NIAAA has awarded grants for training programs to develop personnel especially qualified to deal with American Indian alcoholism. During 1976-1977, thirteen such awards were made to individuals and organizations at a funding level of $1.5 million.[47] For example, the University of California at Berkeley School of Public Health has designed a program to train native Americans to administer, plan, and evaluate Indian alcoholism programs.

Table 4-6
NIAAA Grants, Selected Cities, 1977

City and State	Amount
Salem, Oregon	$128,791
Sacramento, California	119,432
Albuquerque, New Mexico	148,041
Seattle, Washington	178,985
Denver, Colorado	154,000
San Francisco, California	103,000
Dallas, Texas	111,052
Portland, Oregon	123,018
Sioux City, Iowa	85,026
Detroit, Michigan	60,000
Baltimore, Maryland	46,125

Source: Unpublished data provided by the Indian Health Service, 1977.

Trainees can obtain the Master of Public Health degree after twelve to twenty-one months of course work, including seminars on alcoholism within the context of native American culture. Treatment, prevention, and issues of social policy are considered in depth.[48]

Most state alcoholism programs are under the umbrella of mental health activities and according to the American Indian Policy Review Commission Task Force on Alcoholism do not receive planning or funding priority. State alcoholism and mental health programs distribute formula grant funds on the basis of population and not on the basis of need. The Indian is sometimes identified as a special target group, but rarely do funding priorities result in significant assistance.

Many state officials feel that the federal government should have total responsibility for Indian social services (whether urban or rural). They feel that since Indian programs are funded by the NIAAA, it is unnecessary to allocate any resources to deal with the problem of Indian alcoholism.

Case Studies

Most major cities with large Indian populations have alcoholism treatment programs specifically for native Americans. The Baltimore program to be described below is typical of the nonresidential treatment programs that are funded by NIAAA.

Once funding was obtained, the project was staffed by three area residents hired as counselors, with one person appointed coordinator. Two of the three counselors were graduates of the Baltimore City Health Department's Alcoholism Counselor Training Program and the other was the pastor of the largest Indian church in the area. All the staff, including the secretary, were Indians, except for one native Hawaiian.[49]

The program involved the following:

Education of the entire community concerning the overall extent and nature of alcoholism in the immediate area. Methods which were used included: (1) group meetings, (2) use of audio and visual aids, (3) personal testimony, and (4) circulation of printed material.

Prevention of disease among young people and other potential users of alcohol by: (1) encouraging abstinence, (2) reducing the amount of consumption, and (3) teaching socially acceptable drinking habits.

Treatment of those already diagnosed as problem drinkers or abusers of alcohol, through a system aimed at the entire family, by: (1) counseling individuals and groups, (2) referrals to treatment centers, (3) direct intervention and guidance, and (4) follow-up.

According to the first annual report, 941 people were reached during the program's first year of activities.[50] They included: 106 ongoing clients, 383 attendees of eight community colleges, 257 walk-in voluntary self referrals, and 177 outreach clients.

At the close of the first program year, five males and one female who were receiving supporting services from the program staff had been completely sober for five months or more.

It is highly unlikely that the three-year demonstration project will result in stabilizing or diminishing the incidence of Indian alcoholism in Baltimore. To accomplish this goal, a long-term program with significantly greater funding than $46,000 annually (thereby reaching a larger number of problem drinkers) is required.

In Chicago and Los Angeles alcoholism programs are operated for Indians who live in the skid row area of the city. The programs provide food, counseling, and referral for detoxification and other forms of treatment, on a drop-in basis. The program in Los Angeles provides daytime sleeping facilities. The counselors are reformed alcoholics. Neither program has had much success in convincing many of these skid row alcoholics to remain sober, but by helping to keep these people alive these activities do provide some hope for the future. The program in Chicago is funded by the Model Cities Program while the one in Los Angeles is funded by the NIAAA.[51]

Chapters of Alcoholics Anonymous continue to function on several Indian reservations although urban Indian drinkers have generally reacted by withdrawal when asked to participate in a racially integrated group in which "confession" of one's drinking behavior is of major importance. Few Indian people suffering the consequences of alcohol abuse have been helped by the traditional medical approach to rehabilitation or through non-Indian chapters of Alcoholics Anonymous.[52]

It has been accepted by nearly all persons who are knowledgeable regarding Indian alcoholism programs that native Americans will not benefit from projects in which the staff or other participants are not predominantly Indian.

For example, Pioneer House is a treatment facility for male problem drinkers operated by the city of Minneapolis. This facility has consistently shown a high success rate (nearly 50 percent) in working with problem drinkers. However, this facility has had very limited success when working with Indian clientele. Estimates by counselors of the number of native Americans who have maintained sobriety after leaving the center range from one to six.[53]

The other major type of treatment program for Indians involves treatment in a residential setting. The Mendocino State Hospital, which serves alcoholic Indians living in northern California (with a large concentration from the San Francisco Bay region) developed a separate residential program for Indians that was physically segregated from the rest of the hospital alcoholism program.

At Mendocino the use of disulfiram has been strongly encouraged.[54] The policy was adopted to help Indians counteract social pressure to drink when away from the hospital. Savard, for example, has pointed out that Navajos who were trying to remain abstinent frequently lapsed because of pressure from friends to continue drinking.[55] Placing the burden of abstinence on a drug or another person seemed to ease the external and internal conflicts.

Although the Indian patients strongly rejected the use of disulfiram initially, they gradually began approaching the staff surreptitiously to obtain the drug. Eventually, its use was openly accepted by the group.

It soon became evident that large group meetings of patients were not successful in encouraging them to discuss their drinking problem. Indian reluctance to participate was due to the following: (1) generally low self-esteem which resulted in a feeling that one's own comments would be useless; (2) feelings of powerlessness, or a belief that no matter what one said no one really cared to listen and take appropriate action; and (3) a belief that to pursue an active leadership role would result in ostracism from the other patients.

The value of small group sessions was variable. Some group leaders reported that their sessions were beneficial, others had trouble with attendance and never really felt that there was any patient involvement. The groups that seemed to function best were those in which the members had known each other previously and had chosen to be in a group together.

Individual therapy was most successful in terms of patients' willingness to discuss their own problems and accept feedback from the staff. Individual therapy was limited due to a lack of trained therapists, however, and only patients requesting it were given therapy.[56]

Most residential treatment programs for Indian alcoholics have a capacity of 20-40 persons who remain there for 30-60 days. A far larger number are treated by other programs at a significantly lower cost per person. It is not clear that residential treatment programs have a higher success rate than other efforts.

Unless the success rate of residential treatment programs is greater than that obtained by other methods, the former cannot be economically justified. A cost effectiveness analysis of the various kinds of urban Indian alcoholism treatment programs is badly needed.

Summary

Urban Indians face a variety of access barriers to health and medical care. These include language, financial resources, and lack of knowledge regarding existing facilities.

In response to the need for care among urban native Americans, health clinics have been established in most cities with large Indian populations. These clinics have often depended on a volunteer staff and private donations. However, the Indian Health Care Improvement Act has provided limited funding for urban Indian health programs.

The health status of urban Indians is very poor. It may even be worse than the health status of reservation Indians who receive comprehensive free medical services from the IHS. It is important to develop an adequate data base regarding the health status of urban Indians so that funding can be channeled into the areas of greatest need.

Alcoholism is a major Indian health problem. A variety of factors associated with urban Indian alcoholism were discussed, but these should be considered tentative; little empirical research has been done regarding the causes and extent of urban Indian alcoholism.

Several approaches to dealing with the problem of alcoholism were considered—outpatient treatment, "drop-in" centers on skid row, and residential treatment facilities. Lack of evaluation makes it impossible to determine which method is most efficient in terms of the success rate and cost. What is known, however, is that Indians will not respond to alcoholism programs in which the attending staff and patients are predominantly non-Indian.

Notes

1. Task Force Six on Indian Health, *Final Report to the American Indian Policy Review Commission* (Washington, D.C.: U.S. Government Printing Office, 1976), p. 142.

2. U.S. Department of Health, Education, and Welfare, Public Health Service, "Implementation Plan for Title V of the Indian Health Care Improvement Act, Public Law 94-437" (1977), mimeographed, p. 1.

3. Task Force Eight on Urban and Rural Non-Reservation Indians, *Final Report to the American Indian Policy Review Commission* (Washington, D.C.: U.S. Government Printing Office, 1976), p. 72.

4. U.S. Department of Health, Education, and Welfare, "Implementation Plan for Title V," p. 1.

5. Interview with Mr. Wes Halsey, Indian Health Service, July 1977.

6. Ibid.

7. See for example, U.S. Department of Health, Education, and Welfare, Public Health Service, *Indian Health Trends and Services, 1974 Edition* (Rockville, Maryland: Indian Health Service, 1974). Extensive data are available for reservation Indians concerning birth rates, death rates, mortality and morbidity rates from major diseases or conditions, as well as statistics regarding utilization of hospitals, nursing, family planning services, and pharmacies.

8. Task Force Six, *Final Report,* p. 148.

9. American Indian Health Service of Chicago, Inc., "Total Adult and Pediatric Findings Through Clarendon Medical Center, September 1, 1975-June 22, 1976," mimeographed, pp. 1-3. Reservation Indians also have high morbidity rates from these diseases.

10. Ibid., p. 4.

11. Charles McCreary, Charles Deegan, and David Thompson, "Indian Health in Minnesota," *Minnesota Medicine* 56, no. 2 (October 1973):87.

12. David Thompson, "A Sampler of Health Statistics on Minnesota Indians" (no date), unpublished.

13. McCreary, Deegan, and Thompson, "Indian Health in Minnesota," pp. 87-88.

14. Gerard Littman, "Alcoholism, Illness, and Social Pathology Among American Indians in Transition," *American Journal of Public Health and the Nation's Health* 60, no. 9 (September 1970):1773.

15. Minnesota Advisory Committee to the U.S. Commission on Civil Rights, *Bridging the Gap: The Twin Cities Native American Community* (Minneapolis, Minnesota: Minnesota Advisory Committee, 1975), p. 80.

16. League of Women Voters of Minnesota, *Indians in Minnesota* (St. Paul, Minnesota: League of Women Voters, 1974), p. 111.

17. James Uehling, "The Dallas Inter-Tribal Center Clinic: A Health Care Delivery System for American Indians" (1977), mimeographed, p. 1.

18. Willy DeGeyndt and Linda Sprague, "Health Behavior and Health Needs of American Indians in Hennepin County" (Minnesota Training Center for Community Programs, June 2, 1971), p. 23.

19. David Thompson, Anthony Miraglia, and Calvin Iceman, "Health and Mobility Survey of Reservation Indians" (Indian Health Board of Minneapolis, Inc., January 1975), mimeographed, pp. 3, 6, and 7.

20. Michael Fuchs and Rashid Bashshur, "Use of Traditional Indian Medicine Among Urban Native Americans," *Medical Care* 13 (November 1975):926.

21. American Indian Health Service of Chicago, Inc., "Program Narrative" (1975-1976), mimeographed, p. 5.

22. Interview with Ms. Nareen Smith, Indian Health Board of Minneapolis, August 15, 1977.

23. Dallas Department of Public Health, "Dallas Indians Prefer Own Medical Clinic" (1977), mimeographed.

24. Ibid.

25. F.R. Harris and L. Harris, *Indian Health Sources: A Blue Cross Report in the Health Problems of the Poor* (Chicago: Blue Cross, 1968).

26. U.S. Department of Health, Education, and Welfare, *Alcoholism: A High Priority Health Problem* (Washington, D.C.: U.S. Government Printing Office, 1977), DHEW Publication No. (HSA) 77-1001, p. 5.

27. Task Force Eleven on Alcohol and Drug Abuse, *Final Report to the American Indian Policy Review Commission* (Washington, D.C., August 1976), mimeographed, pp. 23-25.

28. Herbert Lochlear, "American Indian Alcoholism: Program for Treatment," *Social Work* 22, no. 3 (May 1977):203; Maryland State Department of Health and Mental Hygiene, "Fact Sheet on Alcoholism in Maryland" (1972), mimeographed.

29. Task Force Eleven, *Final Report,* p. 24.

30. Frances Ferguson, "The Peer Group and Problem Drinking" (Paper presented at the First Annual Meeting of the Southern Anthropological Society, New Orleans, Louisiana, April 7-8, 1966, mimeographed).

31. R.C. Dailey, "Alcohol and the North American Indian: Implications for the Management of the Problems," North American Association of Alcoholism Programs, Paper presented at the 17th Annual Meeting (1966), mimeographed; Frances Ferguson, "Navajo Drinking: Some Tentative Hypotheses," *Human Organization* 27 (1968):159-167.

32. E.M. Jellinik, *The Disease Concept of Alcoholism* (New Haven, Connecticut: College and University Press, 1960), pp. 16, 93-99, and 188-189; Omer Stuart, "Questions Regarding American Indian Criminality," *Human Organization* 23, no. 1 (1964):61-66.

33. U.S. Department of Health, Education, and Welfare, *Alcoholism,* p. 6.

34. Littman, "Alcoholism, Illness, and Social Pathology," p. 1779.

35. Braxton M. Alfred, "Blood Pressure Changes Among Navajo Migrants to Denver, Colorado: A Preliminary Analysis," Navajo Urban Relocation Research Report No. 9 (1965), mimeographed.

36. Littman, "Alcoholism, Illness, and Social Pathology," pp. 1780-1781.

37. Dwight B. Heath, "Drinking Patterns of the Bolivian Camba," in D.J. Pittman and C.R. Snyder, eds., *Society, Culture, and Drinking Patterns* (New York: Wiley, 1962), pp. 22-36.

38. Peter B. Field, "A New Cross-Cultural Study of Drunkenness," in Pittman and Snyder, *Society, Culture, and Drinking Patterns,* pp. 48-74; Edwin M. Lemert, "Alcohol Values and Social Control," in Pittman and Snyder, *Society, Culture, and Drinking Patterns,* pp. 553-571; Ozzie Simmons, "The

Socio-Cultural Integration of Alcohol Use," *Quarterly Journal of Studies on Alcohol* 29, no. 1 (1968):152-171.

39. Theodore D. Graves, "Drinking and Drunkenness Among American Indians," in Jack O. Waddell and O. Michael Watson, eds., *The American Indian in Urban Society* (Boston: Little, Brown and Co., 1971), pp. 274-311.

40. Theodore D. Graves, "Alternative Models for the Study of Urban Migration," *Human Organization* 25 (Winter 1966):299.

41. Graves, "Drinking and Drunkenness," p. 292.

42. Ibid., p. 301.

43. Task Force Eleven, *Final Report,* p. 26.

44. Ibid.

45. Ibid., p. 27.

46. American Indian Policy Review Commission, *Final Report* (Washington, D.C.: U.S. Government Printing Office, 1977), p. 374.

47. National Institute of Alcohol Abuse and Alcoholism, "Training Programs for Native Americans Funded by NIAAA" (1977), mimeographed, p. 1.

48. Ibid., p. 2.

49. Lochlear, "American Indian Alcoholism," p. 206.

50. American Indian Study Center, *Annual Report of the Alcoholism Program* (1975), mimeographed.

51. Interview with Mr. Richard Elm, Director St. Augustine's "Drop-In" Center, Chicago; Interview with Miss Lyle Lewis, Winston, Inc., Los Angeles, August 16, 1977.

52. James Shore and Billee Von Fumetti, "Three Alcohol Programs for American Indians," *American Journal of Psychiatry* 128, no. 11 (May 1972):1450-1451.

53. Vern Drilling, "Problems with Alcohol Among Urban Indians in Minneapolis" (University of Minnesota, Training Center for Community Programs, 1970), mimeographed, p. 2.

54. James Kline and Arthur Roberts, "A Residential Alcoholism Treatment Program for American Indians," *Quarterly Journal of Studies on Alcohol* 34 (1973):863.

55. R.J. Savard, "Effects of Disulfiram Therapy on Relationships Within the Navajo Drinking Group," *Quarterly Journal of Studies on Alcohol* 29 (1968):909-916.

56. Kline and Roberts, "Residential Alcoholism Treatment Program," p. 865.

5 Housing and Social Services

Housing problems for Indian families and individuals commence immediately upon their leaving the reservations and rural communities. Some of these difficulties are related to the kind of housing available in rural Indian communities. For example, few reservation Indians have much knowledge regarding the renting or leasing of homes or apartments. Thus, advice about housing problems prior to relocation is not readily available to Indians since most family members and friends living in rural areas are ignorant of urban living conditions. Being unaware of the urban housing market, each Indian family must learn by experience—a situation that proves to be costly and often results in obtaining inadequate housing.

It is not unusual for Indian families to arrive in cities with very limited funds available for housing expenditures. Moreover, because of discriminatory practices by landlords, the large size of families, low Indian incomes, and a general lack of information about housing alternatives, Indians frequently live in substandard and cramped dwellings.[a]

As indicated in table 5-1, urban Indians experience moderate overcrowding at twice the rate for the total urban population and severe overcrowding at three times the rate for the total urban population. Overall, 19 percent of all urban Indians live in moderately or severely overcrowded housing, while only 7 percent of the total urban U.S. population lives under such substandard conditions.

Moreover, many Indian families must forego essential expenditures on utilities or furniture until they can afford them or are able to establish credit. It must be emphasized that these problems and others are occurring at a most crucial period when the head of the household is seeking employment.[1]

When Indian families succeed in finding housing, particularly when it is located in better neighborhoods, they are often persuaded to sign long-term leases which they may not understand. These leases may require them to make costly repairs on rental property even though it is not their legal obligation to do so. Because of a lack of knowledge regarding housing codes, Indian families are often unprotected against such abuses.

Bias and discrimination also inhibit the choice and selection of desirable housing. If housing markets are tight, the Indian family may have a very limited choice of housing. As a result the Indian family may have to accept substandard

---

[a]Testimony at hearings conducted by the American Indian Policy Review Commission indicates that it has not been unusual for Indians to find that upon personal inquiry, all vacant units have already been filled, or that rent payments turn out to be substantially higher than originally expected once the Indian person begins negotiations for housing.

Table 5-1
Housing and Sanitation for Urban and Rural Indians
(in percent)

Housing-Degree of Crowding	Urban		Rural	
	United States	Indians	United States	Indians
1 or less	92.5	81.3	89.9	55.0
1.01 to 1.50 (moderate)	5.7	12.2	7.1	15.4
1.50 or more (severe)	1.9	6.4	3.0	28.6
Sanitation facilities				
Without water	0.3	0.9	8.9	67.4
Without toilet	0.6	8.6	13.6	48.0

Sources: U.S. Department of Commerce, Bureau of the Census, "1970 Census of the Population, Subject Reports: American Indians," PC(2)-1F (Washington, D.C.); U.S. Department of Commerce, Bureau of the Census, 1970 Census of Housing, "Detailed Housing Characteristics, U.S. Summary," HG-1 (Washington, D.C.); U.S. Department of Commerce, Bureau of the Census, *Detailed Housing Characteristics for the United States, Regions, Divisions and States: 1970, Supplementary Report,* HC(S1)-6 (Washington, D.C.: U.S. Government Printing Office).

housing in poor neighborhoods. This means that Indian families must adjust to urban living in areas characterized by high crime rates, poor sanitation, and cramped living conditions. The extent of these problems may cause many individuals to believe that they were better off living in their rural community.

As indicated above, prejudice of landlords is a problem to Indians despite the 1968 Fair Housing Act. Many restrictions discriminate intentionally or unintentionally against the Indian renter: refusing children, limiting number of occupants, refusing to rent to welfare mothers, demanding a "breakage fee" along with advance rent that puts the price out of reach, and stringent credit checks.[2]

Without doubt, this initial period of urban living is generally one of confusion and frustration for Indians.[3] Given limited external support, the Indian often turns to other members of his family for moral and financial assistance, thus placing an additional burden on other families in similar predicaments. When individuals or entire families move in with other members of an immediate or extended family to lower expenses or because of eviction of the former, the situation is worsened by overcrowding, landlord displeasure, and unhealthy living conditions. If all urban family support breaks down, it is not uncommon for the Indian to return to his particular reservation or rural community, only to return to the city later after reservation resources also become depleted.

The transitory nature of a substantial portion of urban Indian populations to and from reservations, and more recently, to and from other urban Indian communities, is a significant characteristic of the urban native population.[4]

Frequent migration to and from rural Indian communities has notably complicated statistical gathering processes including the compiling of accurate information regarding the need for social services among the urban Indian. Indian and non-Indian agencies attempting to service the urban native community find it especially difficult to include this fluid group as part of the permanent population base.

Housing Codes

Finding decent, inexpensive housing is a major problem for all poor people in the cities and is especially hard for American Indians. The poorest segment of the population, Indians have the least to spend on rent and so get the worst of available housing—often buildings slated for demolition. Old apartment buildings with code violations and frequently changing ownerships are where the majority of urban Indians live.

Although most cities with substantial Indian population have housing codes that purport to protect the occupants from health and safety hazards, they are poorly enforced. These codes generally require periodic inspection of all multiple dwellings, but city housing inspection crews are often so shortstaffed that they can only keep up with complaints. Moreover, there are legal loopholes that enable landlords to ignore code rules. For example, houses scheduled for demolition, a considerable resource for poor Indian renters, need not be brought up to housing code standard.

Uncollected garbage, mice, cockroaches, exposed wiring, and debris piled in the yards plague Indian tenants, but they frequently do not complain because of fear of eviction. For example, the St. Paul agency in charge of housing code enforcement acknowledges that Indians do not use the agency and speculates it is because (1) they are not aware of it, (2) Indians are afraid to complain, and (3) Indians are accustomed to poor housing.[5]

Given the shortage of dwellings, buildings constructed in the last century will continue to be a source of inexpensive housing for years to come. Landlords maintain that improvements such as covering exposed pipes would only increase the rent beyond the reach of the poor. In most urban areas the amount of new low-income housing will be very limited. For example, in Minneapolis, 12,500 housing units, mostly low-cost, were taken off the market by urban-renewal and freeway construction over a ten-year period, but only 2,000 new low-cost units were built to replace them, and those were primarily for elderly couples.[6]

Programs which make available information on housing, rental listings, and leasing, provide a necessary first step in relieving some initial housing problems facing newly migrated Indian families. Such programs could be expanded to include activities that provide information regarding direct supplemental grants or loans for housing, housing improvements, and rent supplements.

Indian Housing in Minneapolis and St. Paul—A Case Study

The 1970 census tract information for areas with relatively high Indian population (from 6 to 10.3 percent) is as follows:[7]

1. Most inhabitants (94 percent) live in rental units. For the population as a whole the comparable figures are 50 percent in Minneapolis and 44 percent in St. Paul.
2. Nearly all (87 percent) live in multi-housing units, while in the overall metropolitan area, 35 percent of the population live in structures having two or more units.
3. Over half of the inhabitants (58 percent) pay less than $60 a month with 82 percent paying less than $80 a month. In St. Paul, 29 percent of the renting population paid less than $80 a month compared to only 21 percent in Minneapolis.
4. In these tracts, 7.2 percent of the units were overcrowded (1 to 1½ persons per room), and 1.4 percent were highly crowded (over 1½ persons per room).

A separate study of Minneapolis Indian housing, done by Indians, revealed that 48 percent of the housing units were overcrowded, and 12 percent were highly crowded, out of a sample of 345 households. Rents were 34 percent of total income. There was a turnover rate of 50 percent per year indicating a high degree of transiency. No hot water was found in 1.4 percent of the residences; no water at all in 0.2 percent, and the residents in 10 percent of the households shared a toilet.[8]

Comparing this study with the census tract information, it is clear that not only do Indians live in the worst areas of the city, but have the poorest housing available in those areas.

A third report on Indian housing in Minneapolis sampled about four hundred households. The findings are summarized in table 5-2. As indicated the housing can simply be described as deplorable.

Public housing in Minneapolis is being used increasingly by Indians. In 1968, the League of Women Voters of Minneapolis reported an estimated 1 percent of all public housing units were occupied by Indians.[9] Housing and Redeveloping Authority estimates for 1973 indicate that in eighty-seven family units in projects on the near north side, 9 percent of the dwellers were Indian and about 13 percent of the persons were Indians (thirty-eight families) in scattered housing units in various other parts of the city.[10]

Table 5-2
Summary of Housing Conditions in Minneapolis

Condition	Proportion of Families
Living in multiple dwellings	100%
Dwellings substandard	72
Broken or inoperative doors	36
Broken plaster, light fixtures, inoperative, and broken steps inside and out	75
One useable emergency fire exit in multiple family dwellings	47
Absence of fire extinguisher, or other means to combat fire in multiple family dwellings	82
One or more relatives living in the same family unit in addition to the immediate family	63
Minimal amount of furniture for family use	68
Problems of refrigeration for food preservation, in some cases requiring the use of window sills to store perishable foods	31
Need exterior repairs	75
Need major interior repairs	71

Source: Gregory Craig, Arthur Harkins and Richard Woods, *Indian Housing in Minneapolis and St. Paul* (Minnesota: Training Center for Community Programs, University of Minnesota, July 1969), mimeographed, pp. 3-5.

In 1973, the housing authority in Duluth estimated that Indians occupied 10 percent of the family units. In St. Paul the estimate was 4 percent Indians in sixty-eight family units (approximately 280 people). A culturally significant statistic is that Indians occupy only 0.2 percent of the high-rise elderly units in both St. Paul and Minneapolis. The older generation is very important to Indians, and they are cared for within the family group.[11]

A group of urban Indians concerned about housing needs in Minneapolis joined together in 1970 and developed a $5 million, 212 unit housing complex known as the South High Housing Development.[12] It is part of the Model Cities urban renewal project, funded by a Federal Housing Administration (FHA) insured mortgage. Section 236 of the Federal Housing Act provides money for interest payments as well as rent supplement funds. The land was made available under an urban renewal program.

The rents in 1974 ranged from $83 for an efficiency apartment to $180 for a five-bedroom townhouse for low-income residents. The project has a community center and swimming pool. Forty percent of the residents are Indian.

The project is governed by a council of residents and other groups that have been involved since the beginning.

The Model City Housing program of Minneapolis, which is federally funded, purchases homes, renovates them, and sells them at market value. As of January 30, 1974, they had sold eight of their fifty-three homes to Indians.

The Minneapolis Upper Midwest American Indian Center has been working for several years to provide emergency housing for newly arrived Indian families. Assisted by voluntary contributions from local churches, it leases ten apartments in multi-family public housing projects in Minneapolis as temporary shelter for Indian newcomers who lack other housing sources. Utilities and furnishings are provided. A limit of sixty days is placed on each family's occupany. The center helps to find permanent housing and furnishings. Rent is collected from those who can pay. Finding available housing for recent arrivals remains the program's greatest difficulty.

As mentioned previously, Indian families are quite mobile *within* cities. Often, initial housing is quite unsatisfactory, so that there is a tendency to move into other dwellings when vacancies occur. Moreover, many Indian families are living in bad neighborhoods so they are motivated to find housing in an environment more suitable to their families and especially for their children. Rent payments may initially claim too large a share of the typically low Indian family income, so that over time lower rent units are sought. Difficulties with landlords, perhaps resulting in eviction for nonpayment of rent or other reasons, sometimes necessitate a search for alternative housing. Demolition of housing through programs of urban renewal also results in mobility.[13]

Indian Neighborhoods

In the early stages of migration of Indians to urban areas the Indian population is often scattered, but as the number of Indians increase, the Indian population tends to become concentrated in particular areas of the city. Thus, in Chicago over half of the Indian population resides in a decaying eight-square-mile area known as Uptown, located on the north side. In Los Angeles, Bell Gardens and Huntingdon Park are centers of Indian population, while in Baltimore about 60 percent of the Lumbees live within six blocks of Baltimore Street and another 30 percent within an area of ten to fifteen blocks around Baltimore Street.[14]

The importance of friends and relatives in residential selection, as well as other migration decisions, implies a channelized migration system and the desirability of a familiar social environment.[15] "Channelization, the movement of individuals from particular origins to particular destinations, is an established rural to urban migration process based on kinship ties and interpersonal communication flows between migrants at origin and destination places."[16] Channelization has resulted in the establishment and maintenance of an urban

Indian community as a continuous flow of migrants arrive and replace earlier ones who depart. The urban Indian community reduces the problems or urban adjustment for newly arrived persons. It functions as a buffer between the contrasting urban and reservation environments by providing an area with familiar faces and activities for migrants who reside there. Since most Indian neighborhoods are located in the poorest sections of the city, there are few jobs within the immediate community. Thus, those Indians who reside near their place of employment are located outside of the Indian community. These persons may be sacrificing an American Indian social setting for employment reasons and concomitantly to obtain improved economic status. Thus, social adjustment is facilitated by residing in an urban Indian enclave while economic adjustment is facilitated by residing near a job site.[17]

Achievement of social adjustment obtained by residing in an urban Indian community requires migrant acceptance of the undesirable conditions of the neighborhood: high rate of transiency, competition from other groups for housing and services, substandard housing, limited commercial and shopping area with high prices, few parks and open spaces, and high crime rates. Conditions such as substandard housing, limited shopping alternatives and high prices may be similar to the reservation situation and not cause adjustment problems. However, the high neighborhood mobility rate and competition for housing and services with other groups may cause internal instability.[18]

American Indians are reluctant to accept and interact with other minorities particularly blacks and Spanish-speaking persons. This limits social adjustment to the urban community at large and encourages a retreat into the Indian community that may begin to approximate an "urban reservation."

The depressed employment and economic situation restricts the probability of job success and encourages participation in the public welfare system. Unless migrants obtain employment, the city represents a continuation of reliance on public assistance similar to the reservation situation and reinforces the problem of dependency. Thus success in achieving social goals may hinder long-term adjustment by making Indian communities approximate an "urban reservation"—possibly the worst of two worlds.

Although there are concentrations of Indian population in urban areas, the fraction of the population that is Indian seldom exceeds 20 percent and often no more than 10 percent. However, as indicated above, urban Indians often have minimal contact with non-Indians even if the non-Indians live in the neighborhood.

For example, in Baltimore, the Lumbees are aware that blacks are victims of discrimination. Therefore, the Lumbees do not want to associate with them lest they be labeled as blacks.[b] The Lumbees make special efforts in Baltimore to

---

[b]Many whites in the Baltimore Street-Broadway area regard Lumbees, except for those who can pass as white, as "colored." The Lumbees resent the epitaph "colored" and do not in any way want to be identified with blacks.

74

avoid areas where blacks have apartments. Moreover, Lumbees tend to shun public housing projects because public housing has a heavy black concentration.[19] Table 5-3 indicates some information on Lumbee contact with other racial groups.

In Chicago, slightly over one-half (55.5 percent) of the initial migrant residences are located in the Uptown American Indian community with the remainder dispersed throughout the Chicago area. Sixty percent of the migrants report proximity to either friends, relatives, or employment as the reasons for selecting their first Chicago home (see table 5-4). The Chicago American Indian population is fairly mobile, averaging .45 moves per year or 1 move every 2.2 years.[20]

Uptown is an area approximately eleven blocks wide and nineteen blocks long (3/4 mile by 1½ miles) on the north side of Chicago, about 4½ miles north of the main downtown area. The 1970 census reported approximately four thousand American Indians living in Uptown, but residents and some service providers believe the number of Indians is closer to twelve to sixteen thousand.[21]

The racial composition and backgrounds of Uptown residents are diverse, since blacks, Spanish-speaking persons, Orientals, southern Appalachian whites, and students, in addition to Indians, live there. The area also contains many interracial couples.

Uptown is a depressed neighborhood of small apartment buildings and small

Table 5-3
Lumbee Interaction with Whites and Negroes

No interaction with Negroes	75
Some contact with Negroes	25
Casual relationship	8
Repeated contact	17
Not considered friend	7
Considered friend	10
No contact with whites	0
Some contact with whites	100
Casual relationship	20
Repeated contact	80
Not considered friend	64
Considered friend	16

Source: Mohammod Amanullah, "The Lumbee Indians: Patterns of Adjustment," in *Toward Economic Development of Native American Communities,* A Compendium of Papers Submitted to the Subcommittee on Economy in Government of the Joint Economic Committee, Congress of the United States, volume 1, part 1, Development Prospects and Problems (Washington, D.C.: U.S. Government Printing Office, 1969), p. 282.

Table 5-4
Selection of the Initial Chicago Residence

Reasons	Percent
Close to friends or relatives	37.0
Close to job	24.0
Good home	11.2
Close to public services	9.3
Low rent	3.7
Close to child's school	1.8
Other	13.0

Source: Tony Lazewski, "American Indian Migrant Spatial Behavior as an Indicator of Adjustment in Chicago," in Jerry McDonald and Tony Lazewski, eds., *Geographical Perspectives on Native Americans: Topics and Resources* (Washington, D.C.: Association of American Geographers, Associated Committee on Native Americans, 1976), p. 105.

shops most of which have absentee owners. About one-third of the housing was torn down under urban renewal to make room for a junior college over protests of the residents, and the housing has not been replaced. Much of the population is transient, unemployment is high, and there are a number of storefront day-labor offices. Elevated railway tracks run over the area.

In Los Angeles there are two principal areas of Indian residence. One is a low-rent area approximately four miles just west of the city center. This area is bounded by Western Avenue, Beverly Boulevard, Figueroa Street, and Pico Boulevard. This area is a place of initial location for Indian families. It has a number of old two- and three-story wooden houses which have been divided into small dwelling units. In this area several Indian churches and a number of Indian bars are located.

The other area of relatively concentrated residence is the small city of Bell Gardens, several miles south and east of the city center. This area was originally, and still is, largely populated by whites from Oklahoma, Arkansas, and Texas. Two Indian churches are located there, including the Indian Revival Center (Assembly of God) which is the largest and most active Indian congregation in the Los Angeles area. This is a working-class community, with small bungalows ten to thirty years old, and a few trailer courts and one-story court-apartment complexes. The Oklahoma-Anglo character is still well preserved, as is indicated by the abundance of fundamentalist Protestant churches.

There is a good deal of transiency in this area. The schools report about a 50 percent change in the school population in a given year. There is some in-migration of Mexican Americans, but whites are also coming into the community. The Indian population has come partly because of the Bureau of Indian Affairs relocation program (which places participants in housing there), but also because churches attract a stable working class Indian group from other parts of the metropolitan area.[22]

Since the earliest arrival of Lumbees in Baltimore, the primary concentration of Indian residence has been East Baltimore. The main center now runs along East Baltimore Street as the east-west axis and is bounded by Broadway on the west, Patterson Park Avenue on the east, Fayette Street to the north, and Pratt Street on the south. The east-west area covers six blocks along East Baltimore Street, and two blocks both north and south of that axis. White people in this central area often seem to be of Appalachian background but there are also present residents of white "ethnic" backgrounds: Italian, Polish, and other Slavic nationalities, and some Greek families.

This is a blighted area. Houses are old. At one time, a number of the houses were one family dwellings and often owner-occupied. But by 1960, many houses had been partitioned into several dwelling units, and the 1960 census found 40 percent of the housing in the area either "deteriorating" or dilapidated—by 1970 the situation was far worse.

Some of the Indians in this area are homeowners but most of them are tenants. They occupy the apartments and furnished rooms that are typical of most of the dwelling units. A good many of the rented houses and apartments are in poor condition, badly in need of paint, littered with broken plaster, and containing bathroom and kitchen fixtures that frequently break down.[23]

Social Services

Urban natives are often recent arrivals facing several stressful transitions simultaneously: from rural to urban, from one culture to another, and from a situation where Indians formed the major share of the community's population to one in which they are a small minority. The urban transition of American Indians is accompanied by serious social problems—poverty, unemployment, underemployment, family disorganization, alcoholism, and other emotional disorders.

Thus, urban migration has greatly augmented the welfare problems of Indians. These individuals are often uninformed about agencies that could help them or are reluctant to seek aid. The human needs of the newly arrived urban Indians and those who have had no success coping with the city are often unknown to the social agencies. These multiple problems appear to be far greater than has been realized.

Federal welfare regulations require 100 percent verification of facts when applying for Aid to Families with Dependent Children (AFDC). This means that all members of the family must have birth certificates as well as other pertinent information, such as marriage certificates and employment and medical records. Those Indians recently arrived in urban areas from reservations or other areas generally don't have these documents with them. Obtaining such information presents problems and takes time, thus delaying the processing of the application for two or three weeks. Meanwhile the families suffer.[24]

In 1969 about 15 percent of all urban Indian families received welfare income. The average amount received was $1,471.[25]

Indians are naturally somewhat reticent and often they will not thoroughly discuss their problems in an interview with someone they don't trust; thus, they are hesitant about seeking services from social agencies which are intended to serve the entire community. Given reluctance to ask for help, and the fact that the agency personnel are often unable to relate to Indians, badly needed assistance in many cases is not being provided. Indians themselves have urged that branch offices of social service agencies be established in areas with a concentration of Indian population and that Indians be hired to meet and work with Indian clients. It is generally accepted that Indians do use programs and agencies that are Indian staffed more readily than is the case when such organizations have no Indian personnel. Moreover, agency staff need special training to better understand the needs of Indians.

Native organizations are frequently established to serve highly specific needs of Indians but not to provide *general* welfare services (see chapter 7). Unfortunately, there does not seem to be a meaningful *linkage* of services between Indian and non-Indian agencies. Therefore, the multiple services available to the rest of the community are often not used or known about by Indian families.[26]

Social service agencies attempt to lessen the social and economic problems of Indians and facilitate the entry of native Americans into the mainstream of society. Jones argues that not only do such agencies frequently fail to achieve such goals but instead foster psychologically and socially deviant reactions among a significant proportion of their clients. She found in Anchorage, Alaska that at least one-third of the native American welfare clients studied, experienced destructive outcomes as a result of their interactions with social agencies.[27]

In Anchorage the proportion of native families receiving public assistance is seven times higher than for whites and four times higher than for blacks.[28]

The characteristics of the social services system that have the most destructive consequences for native American clients include fragmentation of services, the ignorance of agency personnel regarding native American culture, and the lack of planning and evaluation of services provided.

Since social workers are often ineffective (particularly with Indian clients) their agencies cannot risk systematic evaluation of their efforts. This is not to suggest that social agencies evaluate no aspects of their work, but rather than evaluating the effects of their services on clients, agencies evaluate such things as budget management, number of recipients, and use of staff time. These criteria serve as indicators of success which may cover up the reality of widespread failure. In analyzing statistical record keeping in a state employment agency, Blau points out the powerful influence the above evaluation criteria has on workers' behavior and some of the dysfunctions of these criteria.[29]

Social agencies with large resources can pressure other organizations. By failing to refer to agencies that depend on them for referrals, the former have the power to undermine the latter. Thus, the Indian center in Anchorage was nearly put out of business via a "boycott" by established non-Indian social service organizations.

The Anchorage Native Center posed a strong challenge to the existing social services power structure when it assumed a leadership role in organizing a social service planning council without consulting the reorganized and established agency leaders. Some administrators viewed this action as a declaration of intent not to abide by the implicit "rules" of the social service system.

Although it would be impractical under present circumstances for Indian organizations to provide all social services to Indian clients, it is clear that urban social agencies should hire more Indian staff. Moreover, strong linkages need to be established between Indian social service organizations and those that serve the general population.

**Indian Welfare and Poverty Programs in
Minneapolis—A Case Study**

The Hennepin County Welfare Department serves Minneapolis Indians with a variety of public assistance programs, each with specific statutory eligibility requirements. In 1966, 6.4 percent of the families served under the Aid to Families with Dependent Children were Indian. One-third of the state's Indian AFDC families live in Hennepin County.[30] In 1966, 3.3 percent of medical assistance recipients were Indian, and most of these were children known to be "medically deprived." Only 0.4 percent of old age assistance recipients were Indian. This is probably a reflection of the shorter life span of Indians as well as a tendency for many older Indians to return to their home reservation in old age. About 0.7 percent of aid to the disabled recipients were Indian, and 2.1 percent of those receiving aid to the blind were Indian people.

Those clients who do not qualify for categorical assistance are served by the Minneapolis Department of Public Relief. Relief granted by this department is primarily for subsistence and transportation to job interviews and medical facilities.

From 1959-1969 the proportionate representation of Indians on the relief rolls increased over 300 percent from 4 percent of the total population in 1959, to 13 percent in 1969. The percentage of blacks increased about 20 percent from 10.7 to 13 percent. The percentage of white cases declined from 85.3 percent of the total in 1959, to 74 percent in 1969.[31]

A 1972 study by the staff of the Indian Health Board, Minneapolis, indicates the dependency of many city Indians on welfare income. The staff interviewed all Indian households known to them in the inner city. For a group of 389 households, the primary source of income was: AFDC 55 percent, employment 13 percent, and "no sources" 25 percent.[32] It was assumed that the 25 percent were surviving through help from relatives, surplus food stocks, and by work at day-labor jobs.

The Minneapolis Relief Department has one Indian on the staff. He serves in the capacity of alcoholism counselor. The department has made several attempts to recruit Indians through advertising in the newspaper and personal recruiting efforts. Since the annual turnover of caseworkers is about 90 percent, it would be relatively easy to find employment for Indian social workers if they would apply and could qualify.[33]

There are no Indians on the Board of Public Welfare, the policy-making body of the Relief Department. A proposed Indian advisory committee has not been formed because it has been difficult to get people who are willing to serve on such a committee.

One year of residence in Minneapolis is required to qualify for city relief. During that first year, the relief agent for the county of previous residency is responsible for payments. There are two major problems associated with this policy. First, rural based payment scales are less than adequate for subsistence in the city; and secondly, the Bureau of Indian Affairs (the relief agent for Red Lake Reservation) refuses to reimburse the Minneapolis Relief Department.

The county Welfare Department has one Indian employee, a case aide, out of a total of 840 employees. Attempts to recruit Indian staff have been made through the Urban League and Indian leaders. However, these attempts have been unsuccessful.[34]

There are no Indians on the Hennepin County Welfare Board and since it is a position to which one is elected, it is unlikely there will be any in the near future. There is a citizens' advisory committee with twenty-one members, two of whom are Indian.

Urban Indians to some extent share in poverty programs with all citizens. The Pilot City Program in Minneapolis was primarily funded by OEO, but is now financed by the Federal Department of Health, Education, and Welfare (HEW). It has had some Indian staff and a resident advisory committee of Indians. Located in North Minneapolis, it is intended to bring together a number of federal programs in the areas of employment assistance, homemaking aid, and health services.

Another federal program, the Model Cities Program in South Minneapolis, is channeling federal funds into the rehabilitation of a residential area. Funded by the U.S. Department of Housing and Urban Development (HUD) and HEW, the project is directed by a 107-person board of residents elected on a geographical basis that assures minority representation, including Indians. This program provided the funds for building the Urban American Indian Center and the South High Housing Project.[35]

Hennepin County and Minneapolis have not had an antipoverty agency since 1971. Formerly, OEO funded an Indian Citizen Community Center and youth programs.

Child Welfare

The removal of Indian children from their homes by social agencies has reached major proportions. In a recent survey the Association on American Indian Affairs reported that in states with large Indian populations, 25 to 35 percent of all Indian children are removed from their families and placed in foster homes, adoptive homes, or institutions.[36] Jones found that in an Aleut village, social welfare workers, apparently confusing poverty and cultural differences with social deprivation and psychological abuse, removed 19 native children from their homes in a fifteen-month period. This represented nearly one-third of the minor children in the native community.[37] Most of these children were placed in urban foster homes and institutions. This situation most frequently occurs when parents are drinking and the children are seemingly left alone. Often, however, nondrinking friends and relatives watch the children of drinking parents. However, this fact is often unknown to social agency personnel who essentially believe the children have been abandoned.

Foster homes for Indian children are in short supply, as are foster homes generally. There is an increasing feeling (with little hard evidence) that Indian children are better off in Indian homes. There are strong pressures in the Indian community to find Indian alternatives to white foster homes. It is stressed that putting an Indian child into a white home causes the child to lose his identity and become ashamed of being Indian. Because of the lack of placements for Indian adolescents, they are sometimes committed to correctional institutions, while non-Indians would be given alternative treatment for similar offenses.

Meeting state and county standards for foster homes is difficult for Indian people because of low income, poor living conditions, and large families. Greater flexibility of standards for foster homes is needed if Indian children are to be placed in Indian foster homes.

The proportion of Indian child welfare caseloads is far higher than the proportion of Indian children in the total child population of a state. This is indicated in table 5-5 which presents this information for four states in which the majority of Indians are urban Indians.

There are many possible reasons why Indians are overrepresented in the caseloads of state child welfare agencies. Perhaps there is a greater need for services on the part of Indians or perhaps there are inconsistencies between the needs of Indian families and standardized practices for providing child welfare services to the general population.

The persons responsible for making decisions about child neglect may not be equipped by their professional training to decide whether or not a child is suffering emotional damage at home, in spite of conditions which might indicate neglect in a white middle-class home. For example, Indian children are given a

Table 5-5
Child Welfare Caseloads of State Child Welfare Departments

State	Service	Indian Cases	As Percent of Total Caseload	Year of State Figures	Indians Under 18 as Percent of Population (1970 Census)
California	Adoption	17	6.4	1975	0.5
	Family care	353	1.2	1975	
Illinois	Adoption	18	1.3	1974	0.1
	Foster family care	69	0.6	1974	
	Group home care	6	1.5	1974	
	Institution care	6	0.2	1974	
	Social services for children in their own homes	47	0.5	1974	
	Adolescent training and support services	9	0.7	1974	
Minnesota	Adoption decrees	83	2.6	1974	0.8
	Adoption placements	56	4.1	1974	
	Children committed to state guardianship	32	8.1	1974	
	Children under state guardianship	586	25.2	1974	
	Foster family care	733	13.3	1974	
	Group home service	65	7.6	1974	
	Institutional care	79	2.9	1974	
	Residential treatment	49	4.2	1974	
	Social services for children in their own homes	2133	6.7	1974	
	Social services for unmarried mothers	191	6.2	1974	
Wisconsin	Adoptive placements	42	8.2	1970	0.6
	Children under custody of Division of Family Services	288	11.5	1972	
	Foster care—boarding homes	163	14.0	1972	
	Foster care—group homes	10	9.1	1972	

Source: Center for Social Research and Development, University of Denver, *Indian Child Welfare: A State of the Field Study* (1976), mimeographed, pp. 33-34.

great deal more responsibility than is common in other cultures. They may play farther from home, unsupervised by an adult (although older children are usually responsible for the younger ones).[38] Dr. Joseph Westermeyer found that in Minnesota Indian parents leaving young children in the care of eight- or ten-year-old children are charged with abandonment.[39]

Foster care and adoptive and protective services for Indians are primarily provided by county departments of social services, although private, community, or denominational agencies may provide a small percentage of the services.

Indian centers and Indian social services agencies are usually involved in foster care only to the extent of providing caseworkers to families especially prior to removal of a child from the home. Virtually no Indian organizations have a license to place children in foster homes or other case settings. The primary role played by the Indian agencies in adoptions is that of referring unwed mothers and families who wish to adopt to the appropriate agencies. Indian agencies are also involved in recruitment of Indian foster and adoptive families.[40]

Large numbers of Indian children are placed in non-Indian foster homes. Westermeyer found that in Minnesota in 1969 out of over seven hundred foster homes caring for Indian children, only two had an Indian parent.[41] Moreover, a 1974 survey of placements of Indian children in Washington State found that 114 of 159 children were placed in non—Indian homes.[42]

Since 1958 the Bureau of Indian Affairs has contracted with the Child Welfare League of America to operate an interstate adoption exchange for Indian children. From 1958-1975 the project has assisted the adoption of approximately seven hundred American Indian children. The majority of children were placed on the East Coast or in the states of Illinois, Indiana, or Missouri; 90 percent were adopted by non-Indian families.[43]

The Native American Community House of Seattle

The Native American Community House (NACH) is the first urban Indian program of its kind in the United States. It developed from the concern of many members of the Seattle Indian community over the separation of Indian parents from their children in foster care. NACH is run by the Seattle Indian Center. It is set up to be an alternative to foster care for those Indian people who want it.

NACH is based on the belief that families can learn to handle their problems and through such learning stay together. NACH believes that the family problems can be handled with assistance from the Seattle Indian community, and through living in a residential setting under the guidance of a professional staff.

NACH is located in the south end of Seattle. The program operates an apartment building with several individual apartment units. The staff helps organize the resident families for project activities, as well as providing aid with such problems as unemployment, drinking, drug abuse, and child care.

To be eligible for NACH a family must have at least one child under six years of age, enter the program voluntarily, and stay in it for at least three months. In addition, family heads must permit Alternative to Foster Care Project staff (ATFCP) to obtain client records from appropriate Department of Social and Health Services agencies (DSHS) as well as other community agencies.

One of the biggest problems has been to obtain referrals from non-Indian welfare organizations. An administrative directive from the head regional administrator of DSHS to local offices, specifying mode of referral, case transferring, and methods of maintaining contact with the client family and the staff of ATFCP, helped to increase referrals.

A study of twenty-six families resident at the ATFCP indicated that 92 percent were without income or receiving welfare and that the majority already had children taken from their homes (many wanted assistance to get them back). In 85 percent of the cases the mother was the head of the household.[44]

The major criterion for evaluating the effects of the residential program was its success in helping the client families to avert child separation or to regain their children. Sixteen families obtained the return of forty-nine children; two families were unable to obtain return of their three children. Moreover, nine families with thirty-two children stayed together as a family.[45] However, the long-term effect of the program is unclear; 46 percent of the families were involuntarily terminated from the program, primarily for drinking.

The cost per child per month in 1974 of those participating in AFTCP was $94.93 per month compared to $127.52 per month expenditure per child placed in a foster home in Seattle. Given the obvious noneconomic advantage of returning a child to his parents' home or keeping him there, it is interesting to note there is an economic advantage as well.[46]

Summary

Indian housing conditions in cities are very poor. Native Americans live in the worst housing in the most blighted areas of cities. Lack of enforcement of housing codes, landlord prejudice, and ignorance of alternatives all limit the choice of housing available to urban Indians.

There is a tendency for Indians to be concentrated in particular sections of cities. Although this may facilitate social adjustment and ease the transition from the reservation, in the long run it may hinder economic adjustment.

Non-Indian social agencies have had little success with Indian clients. Although it is believed that Indian organizations can accomplish more with native Americans than other agencies, it is not feasible to transfer all the responsibility for Indian social services to the former. What is needed is better

84

linkages between Indian and non-Indian social agencies and more Indian staff for the latter.

The widespread placement of Indian children in non-Indian foster homes is a matter of serious concern. Few Indian organizations have the resources or facilities to place children. The Alternative to Foster Care Project by the Native American Settlement House in Seattle is a useful pilot project in the effort to help Indian families with problems stay together.

Notes

1. Task Force Eight on Urban and Rural Non-Reservation Indians, *Final Report to the American Indian Policy Review Commission* (Washington, D.C.: U.S. Government Printing Office, 1976), p. 69.

2. League of Women Voters of Minnesota, *Indians in Minnesota* (St. Paul: League of Women Voters, 1974), p. 124.

3. Task Force Eight, *Final Report,* p. 70.

4. Ibid.

5. League of Women Voters of St. Paul, "Indian Housing Study Committee Working Papers" (St. Paul: League of Women Voters, March 1973), p. 7.

6. "Many Houses are not 'Homes' in Minnesota," *Minneapolis Tribune* (March 15, 1970).

7. "1970 Census Data (First Count)," Minnesota Analysis and Planning Systems, Census Tract #34 and #61, Minneapolis, #329 St. Paul. Also "Metropolitan Area–1970 Census, Housing Unit Characteristics," Datalog, Metropolitan Council of the Twin Cities Area, St. Paul (October 28, 1971).

8. Upper Midwest American Indian Center (Pilot City), "Urban Indian Housing" (Minneapolis, 1973).

9. League of Women Voters of Minneapolis, and the Training Center for Community Programs, University of Minnesota, *Indians in Minneapolis* (Minneapolis: League of Women Voters, 1968).

10. League of Women Voters of Minnesota, *Indians in Minnesota,* p. 126.

11. Ibid.

12. Ibid.

13. Prafulla Neog, Richard Woods, and Arthur Harkins, *Chicago Indians: The Effects of Urban Migration* (Minnesota: Training Center for Community Programs, University of Minnesota, January 1970), p. 12.

14. Mohammod Amanullah, "The Lumbee Indians: Patterns of Adjustment," in *Toward Economic Development for Native American Communities,* a compendium of papers submitted to the Subcommittee on Economy in Government of the Joint Economic Committee, Congress of the United States, volume 1, part 1, Development Prospects and Problems (Washington, D.C.: U.S. Government Printing Office, 1969), p. 282.

15. Tony Lazewski, "American Indian Migrant in Chicago," in Jerry McDonald and Tony Lazewski, eds., *Geographical Perspectives on Native Americans: Topics and Resources* (Washington, D.C.: Association of American Geographers, 1976), p. 106.

16. John S. MacDonald and Beatrice MacDonald, "Chain Migration, Ethnic Neighborhood Formation and Social Networks," *Milbank Memorial Fund Quarterly* 42 (1963):85.

17. Lazewski, "American Indian Migrant," p. 109.

18. Ibid., p. 114.

19. Amanullah, "The Lumbee Indians," p. 293.

20. Lazewski, "American Indian Migrant," p. 112.

21. Center for Social Research and Development, University of Denver, *Indian Child Welfare: A State of the Field Study* (Denver, 1976), mimeographed, p. 203.

22. Estelle Fuchs and Robert Havighurst, *To Live on This Earth: American Indian Education* (Garden City, New York: Doubleday, 1972), pp. 278-279.

23. Abraham Makofsky, *Tradition and Change in the Lumbee Indian Community of Baltimore* (Catholic University of America, Ph.D. dissertation, 1971), pp. 52-57.

24. League of Women Voters of Minnesota, *Indians in Minnesota,* p. 82.

25. U.S. Department of Commerce, Bureau of the Census, 1970 Census of Population, *American Indians* (Washington, D.C.: U.S. Government Printing Office, 1973), p. 120.

26. Community Health and Welfare Council, *Services to Urban American Indians* (Minneapolis, April 1974), mimeographed, p. 13.

27. Dorothy M. Jones, *The Urban Native Encounters the Social Service System* (Alaska: Institute of Social Economic and Government Research, University of Alaska, 1974), p. 2.

28. Ibid., p. 14.

29. Peter Blau, *The Dynamics of Bureaucracy: A Study of Interpersonal Relations in Two Government Agencies* (Chicago: University of Chicago Press, 1963), pp. 36-55.

30. League of Women Voters of Minneapolis and the Training Center for Community Programs, University of Minnesota, *Indians in Minneapolis* (Minneapolis: League of Women Voters, April 1968), p. 2.

31. Richard Woods and Arthur Harkins, *A Review of Recent Research on Minneapolis Indians, 1968-1969* (Minnesota: University of Minnesota, Training Center for Community Programs, December 1969), p. 22.

32. Indian Health Board of Minneapolis, *Progress Report* (1973), mimeographed.

33. League of Women Voters of Minneapolis, *American Indians and Minneapolis Public Services* (Minneapolis: League of Women Voters, 1971), mimeographed, p. 30.

34. Ibid., p. 32.

35. League of Women Voters of Minnesota, *Indians in Minnesota,* p. 92.

36. Association on American Indian Affairs, Inc., "Family Defense," *Bulletin of the Association on American Indian Affairs, Inc.,* no. 1 (Winter 1974):1.

37. Dorothy M. Jones, "Child Welfare Problems in an Alaskan Native Village," *Social Service Review* 43, no. 3 (1969):297-309.

38. Joseph J. Westermeyer, "Indian Powerlessness in Minnesota," *Society* 50 (1973):4.

39. Ibid., p. 50.

40. Center for Social Research and Development, *Indian Child Welfare,* p. 148.

41. Ibid.

42. Hideki A. Ishisaka, "Evaluation Report: Alternative to Foster Care," Project of the Seattle Indian Center, Inc. Grant No. OCD-CB-397-C2 from the U.S. Department of Health, Education, and Welfare, Office of Child Development (Seattle: Seattle Indian Center, 1975), p. 2.

43. David Fanshel, *Far From the Reservation: The Transracial Adoption of American Indian Children* (Metuchen, New Jersey: Scarecrow Press, 1972), pp. 34-35; and Center for Social Research and Development, *Indian Child Welfare,* p. 273.

44. Ishisaka, "Evaluation Report," pp. 36 and 39.

45. Ibid., p. 70.

46. Ibid., p. 83.

6 Urban Indian Education

Despite the deplorable conditions which exist at some of the Indian schools located on or near the reservations,[1] the students enrolled there enjoy at least two advantages over their urban counterparts. In the boarding, day, and mission schools on the reservations, the number of Indian students is normally large and students have fellow natives with whom they can identify. In recent years, a relaxation of attitudes has also occurred among school administrators and some aspects of Indian culture are now taught or permitted in the classroom. For example, students may be allowed to take Indian beadwork classes or to enjoy a course in leather goods where moccasin making would be learned.[2]

In contrast, the number of Indian children in urban classrooms is generally very small. For example, in Baltimore the proportion of the student body that is Indian is 10 percent at one elementary school, 1.5 percent at one junior high, and less than 0.5 percent at one high school; in Los Angeles no school had a population more than 2 percent Indian; in Chicago elementary and junior high schools had 1 to 5 percent Indian pupils.[3] In addition, the school system is oriented to emphasize the values and attitudes of the dominant culture.

In the fall of 1970, about 13 percent of the Indian pupils attending public schools were in the large cities (100,000 or more population).[a] Nine urban areas accounted for over half the Indian enrollment in major cities (see table 6-1).

The cultural pattern exhibited by Indians is quite different from that of non-Indian pupils. Indian children are said to be:[4]

1. Oriented to the present rather than the future;
2. Fearful and distrustful of unknown situations, rather than confident and gregarious;
3. Generous rather than covetous;
4. Considerate of feelings of individuality rather than inconsiderate and interfering; and
5. Cooperative rather than competitive.

Each of the traits enumerated above is nearly the opposite of those valued most highly by white society. When the native American child is placed in the urban classroom he quickly learns that most of his teachers and fellow students have a very different cultural orientation. It is not surprising that the Indian child should experience feelings of confusion and frustration.

---

aHowever, a total of 130,000 off-reservation Indians attend public schools, mostly in towns and small and medium-size cities.

Table 6-1
Indian Student Population, Selected Cities, 1970

City	Number of Indians Enrolled	Percent of Total City Enrollment
Tulsa, Oklahoma	2,435	3.1
Oklahoma City, Oklahoma	2,413	3.4
Minneapolis, Minnesota	1,985	3.0
Albuquerque, New Mexico	1,827	2.2
Los Angeles, California	1,123	0.2
Chicago, Illinois	1,042	0.2
Seattle, Washington	827	1.0
Phoenix, Arizona	801	2.0
Milwaukee, Wisconsin	726	0.5

Source: National Center for Educational Statistics, "The American Indian in School: Answers to Questions–Advance Statistics for Management," *Bulletin* no. 13 (January 1973): 9.

Additional problems may result from the fixed time schedules and rigid classroom discipline imposed upon students in an urban classroom. Native Americans do not generally consider time in terms of minutes and hours and are generally less concerned about maintaining strict schedules. In most aspects of their lives they also favor flexibility over rigidity.

As part of a study of the education of Cherokee Indians in eastern Oklahoma, Petit and Wax focused on an elementary school in Tulsa. This school, which contained some 10 percent Indian pupils, is considered by the investigators as illustrative of the kind of school to which rural northeast Oklahoma Indians migrating to Tulsa might send their children.[5]

The Tulsa school experienced the problems of many inner city schools elsewhere—older plant, poor tax base causing continued financial difficulties, and central administration of hiring and firing. There was preoccupation with discipline and order. Many teachers lacked experience, and there was a high turnover rate among teachers.

A study of a Minneapolis junior high school attended by Indian children reported similar conditions. In addition, the investigators found that Indian parents had minimal contact with the school, and that there was a lack of human and professional concern for Indian students on the part of a significant number of classroom teachers. Many teachers were apparently ignorant of Indian lifestyles and showed little evidence that they were willing to make meaningful contact with their Indian students.[6]

Traditionally, Indians learn and are taught in a manner that is different from that employed in most classrooms. In a typical learning situation, the native

American child or adult engages in an extended period of observation. He attempts a task himself only when he feels comfortable with it and failure seems unlikely. This is in marked contrast to the teaching methods generally employed by non-Indian instructors which emphasize public practice and preliminary awkward attempts at problem solving. Both of these methods of learning can be embarrassing and threatening for the Indian student.

As indicated in chapter 5, most large urban areas contain native American families who have resided in one location for several years; likewise, there are families who move within the city limits and back and forth from the reservation with great frequency. This transiency clearly affects the student's attendance and academic achievement, as well as his ability to socialize and feel secure.

In some cases, Indian youngsters are needed at home and, therefore, are removed from school while a family crisis exists. Because of poor attendance records, many of these otherwise conscientious students have repeated contact with truant officers, a situation which does little to help the student or improve Indian attitudes toward the educational system.

The Indian child studying in the urban classroom will probably be taught little that will enhance his self-concept. Most existing textbooks generally emphasize non–Indian values and concepts. The Indian student learns very little that is good about Indian people as a whole and probably nothing about his own particular tribe. There is a great lack of Indian-related teaching materials in the urban school system. Moreover, most non-Indian teachers have little knowledge about contemporary Indians or where one would obtain information concerning them. Since most urban teachers seldom encounter or teach native Americans, such ignorance is quite understandable.

Urban Indian Dropout Rates

One of the most crucial problems in urban Indian education is the high dropout rate. Probably less than a third of urban Indian students complete high school. In some cities the native American dropout rate reaches 80-90 percent.

A number of factors have been cited as causes of the high dropout rate among urban Indians:

1. Teacher insensitivity to native Americans as individuals and as members of a unique culture;
2. Peer group hostility and prejudice;
3. School curricula which ignore the strengths of Indian culture and emphasize white middle-class values; and
4. The lack of native American staff in the school system and its attendant effect on the self-concept of Indian students.

Although there is a belief among Indian parents that a high school education can be useful and is sometimes necessary, family lifestyles may inhibit school attendance and achievement. As mentioned previously, kinship and family obligations frequently require the child to stay home and look after the house or watch younger siblings while both parents are away. Poverty also contributes to a lack of money for lunch or, especially for the older children attending high school, the lack of money to purchase appropriate clothing; children may need to leave school and find a job to help support the family. Frequent moves among the more transient Indians, accompanied by school transfers, also contribute to difficulties in school and subsequently there is a high probability that the student will drop out.

In addition, there is a strong tendency for academic learning and self-achievement to be considered unimportant among Indians or even inappropriate behavior. Such activity involves putting oneself above others. Indian youth or young adults, especially after they have attended college, are aware of the difference between traditional Indian values and those of the dominant society. They realize that difficulties would ensue in terms of personal relationships if they returned to their home communities (which many would like to do to improve conditions). They experience a growing sense of altruism but are frustrated by the realization that alienation from the Indian community may be the price they paid for obtaining an education.[7]

It is unfortunate that Indians are moving to cities at precisely the time that many urban centers are in a state of advanced decay. Relocating for jobs, the Indians face growing unemployment; in terms of education, their children face the difficulties of the inner city schools; in housing they are faced with slums and displacement by urban renewal.

Disappointment with urban living and schools is likely to affect many Indian youngsters. The continued existence of the BIA reservation boarding-school system represents a possible alternative for those seeking special programs and an environment different from that of urban schools.

Economic Considerations

One possible reason for the high dropout rate among urban Indian youth could be the fact that economic success is not enhanced by additional years of schooling.[b] Thus, if urban Indian high school graduates earn little more than dropouts, there is minimal economic incentive to complete secondary school.

Wilber and Hagan, using a national sample of Indians (surveyed in the 1970 census), found a positive relationship between earnings and education in four regions of the country where a majority of Indians are urban Indians (see table 6-2).

[b]In terms of the theory of investment in human capital, this is equivalent to stating that the rate of return on investment in secondary education is relatively low.

Table 6-2

Proportion of Indians Earning More Than $3,500, Selected Regions, Males and Females

Region	Males		Females	
	Dropout	Graduate	Dropout	Graduate
New Jersey, New York	65	79	35	59
Delaware, Maryland, D.C., Pennsylvania, Virginia, West Virginia	63	–	25	50
Illinois, Indiana, Michigan, Minnesota, Ohio, Wisconsin	73	82	31	50
Arizona, California, Nevada	62	76	29	46

Source: George Wilber and Robert Hagan, *Minorities in the Labor Market,* Volume III (Kentucky: Social Welfare Research Institute, University of Kentucky, 1975), mimeographed, p. 87.

Thus, as indicated, earnings of urban male Indian high school graduates are greater than for dropouts; however, the relationship is even stronger for females. One reason why earnings of urban Indian high school graduates are higher than dropouts is that the former are less likely to be unemployed. Although no national data are available concerning the overall relationship between education and unemployment, a comprehensive employment survey in Chicago revealed some information (see table 6-3).

The other reason why the earnings of urban Indians with high school education are greater than dropouts is that the former have more skilled jobs. Data from the Wilber and Hagan study cited above indicates that the mean occupational score for urban Indian high school graduates is higher than the mean occupational score for Indian dropouts (see table 6-4).

If education reduces the probability of urban Indian unemployment, and permits one to obtain a more skilled job and thereby increases income, why is the Indian dropout rate so high? Obviously economic incentives are not working or they are counterbalanced by the noneconomic considerations mentioned previously. However, in the final analysis at least part of the blame must be placed on Indian parents. Indian parents do not motivate their children to attend school or to remain in school. Many are ambivalent about the benefits of "non-Indian" education since their own experiences may have been negative. If parents do not actively encourage their children to attend school or remain there, and if the child's peer group expresses little interest in education, the child is more likely to drop out.

Table 6-3
Education and Unemployment, Chicago Indians

Years of School Completed	Unemployment Rate
0	41.7%
1-7	36.0
8	33.3
9-11	44.2
12	30.7
13-15	26.0
16 and over	16.8

Source: John K. White, "Patterns in American Indian Employment: A Study of the Work Habits of American Indians in Chicago, Illinois" (Chicago, Illinois: St. Augustine's Indian Center, 1971), mimeographed.

United States Office of Education Programs

As citizens of the United States and of the states where they reside, Indian people are eligible for all the programs operated by the United States Office of Education provided the criteria for funding eligibility set by each program are satisfied. At present, according to data compiled by the United States Office of Education (USOE) of approximately 110 programs funded by that agency, Indian people participate in or receive benefits from only 40. The level of funding for these latter programs amounts to $167 million, or 2.4 percent of the agency's budget for 1975 (see table 6-5).

However, these figures are only approximate. One important reason for the imprecision regarding funding levels is that the various programs have different definitions of the term Indian. For example, the Indian Education Act defines Indian with sufficient breadth to include all federally and nonfederally recognized tribes, as well as terminated, rural, and urban Indians. Other programs use the BIA definition of Indian (one-quarter or more Indian blood); still others use state definitions or definitions developed by the individual program office. Since many programs are funded on a per capita basis, eligibility definitions directly affect the total allocation.

Moreover, many of the programs that allocate funds on behalf of Indians do so via projects that assist several ethnic groups simultaneously. Although administrators recognize many of these grants serve multi-ethnic populations, they have no adequate information to estimate the actual level of Indian participation in these programs. Since it is not possible to determine the proportion of the total grant award that is spent on Indian participants, the entire funding allocation is considered to be of benefit to Indians.

Table 6-4

Mean Occupation Score, Indians, Selected Regions, Males and Females

	Males		Females	
Region	Dropout	Graduate	Dropout	Graduate
New Jersey, New York	32	40	19	26
Delaware, Maryland, D.C., Pennsylvania, Virginia, West Virginia	30	39	19	26
Illinois, Indiana, Michigan, Minnesota, Ohio, Wisconsin	30	37	20	23
Arizona, California, Nevada	29	34	17	20

Source: George Wilber and Robert Hagan, *Minorities in the Labor Market*, Volume III (Kentucky: Social Welfare Research Institute, University of Kentucky, 1975), mimeographed, p. 87.

The quality and quantity of data available within a program to compute the allocation to Indians varies. For example, regarding the discretionary grant programs, it can sometimes be determined whether or not the grant serves Indian people from the application form and grant narratives. If the program is funded through entitlements or block grants to the states, the information concerning Indian participation is meager. Because the Office of Management and Budget (OMB) has limited data collection efforts, these programs have no authority to extend or update their current data bases. To compute statistics concerning services to Indians, administrators must usually contact each state program office. These state officials must then decide whether or not to provide federal personnel with data. Unfortunately, OMB will usually not approve program application or reporting forms that request a distribution of number of participants by race. If the state departments receiving such funds do not keep data on Indian participation in federal projects, the program's statistics may be little more than extrapolations of possible levels of Indian enrollment.[8]

Factors Inhibiting the Impact of USOE Funding

The actual allocation of funds to local educational agencies or other service entities within a state are made by the state Department of Education or equivalent administrative unit. Even though Indians may be legally eligible for services from such programs, the determination as to whether they will benefit

Table 6-5

Estimate of United States Office of Education Expenditures that Benefit Indians or Are Attracted by the Presence of Indians, 1975

(thousands)

Program and Program Objectives	Expenditures
Elementary and secondary education	$ 50,837
Indian Education Act	42,000
School assistance in federally affected areas	
Emergency school aid	35,862
Education for the handicapped	3,432
Occupational, vocational and adult education	1,221
Higher education	8,330
Library Resources	24,476
Total	167,261

Source: Helen Scheirbeck, Earl Barlow, Lorraine Misiasyck, Kathy McKee, and Kyle Patterson, Task Force Five on Indian Education, *Final Report to the American Indian Policy Review Commission* (Washington, D.C.: U.S. Government Printing Office, 1976), pp. 93-97.

or not is generally made by the state Department of Education. Thus, while Indians may be eligible for services from such programs, they may not benefit from such expenditures unless the state is actively concerned with Indian education. Indian school-age children are often widely scattered through the state's school districts. Thus, the state Department of Education would have to target money into each local educational agency in which Indian children are enrolled to insure that all Indian children participated in federally supported program classes and activities.

Moreover, most Indian communities (whether urban or rural) lack the skilled professionals in the fields of educational planning and administration to meet the needs regarding the preparation of grants and management of the grant awards. For example, in the area of library services, there are less than one hundred native Americans who are professional librarians. These Indian communities would have a hard time competing with others for available federal funding.

Finally, program decisions with USOE generally are made on the basis of national trends. Such data are often not indicative of the situation in Indian communities. National statistics, for example, indicate a surplus of teachers available for employment. As a result, USOE programs that provide teacher training funds have shifted their funding emphasis to retraining or inservice training. This has had an adverse effect on Indian communities who had relied heavily on such programs to help fill their critical need for native American teachers.[9]

The Indian Education Act

The Indian Education Act (IEA) of 1972 (Title IV of Public Law 92-318) is concerned with the public elementary and secondary education of Indian children and to some extent native American adult education. The legislation has four major provisions.

Part A is intended to provide financial assistance to local educational agencies to develop and implement supplementary educational programs designed to meet the special needs of Indian students. State and local jurisdictions are cautioned not to think of these funds as a substitute for their own financial support of education. Thus, states and localities are prohibited from reducing their level of expenditures by more than 5 percent.

Part B authorizes a series of broad grant programs for special projects and programs aimed at improving educational opportunities for Indian children. Such grants can be used for bilingual and bicultural programs, special health and nutrition services, remedial and compensatory instruction, and comprehensive guidance, counseling, and testing services.

Part C focuses on adult education. The definition of "adult" is flexible and includes school dropouts, who are often quite young. Projects funded under part C can include: programs to stimulate provision of basic literacy opportunities to all adult nonliterate Indian adults; programs to provide opportunities for Indian adults to obtain a high school equivalency certificate; and programs to develop better techniques for attaining high school equivalency and employability.

Part D provides for the establishment of the Office of Indian Education within the U.S. Office of Education.[10]

The level of funding for the various sections of this legislation is given in table 6-6. This act is the only legislation within USOE which encourages the study of Indian culture, in addition to traditional academic subjects. The former is supported to reinforce pride in Indian heritage and to create a more satisfying

Table 6-6
Levels of Funding Indian Education Act

	1975	1976	1977
Part A	$25,000,000	$35,000,000	$42,055,000
Part B	12,000,000	16,000,000	12,000,000
Part C	3,000,000	4,000,000	3,000,000
Part D	1,804,000	1,825,000	2,055,000
Total	$41,804,000	$56,825,000	$59,110,000

Source: National Advisory Council on Indian Education, *Fourth Annual Report to the Congress of the United States* (Washington, D.C.: U.S. Government Printing Office, 1977), p. 61.

relationship between the Indian child and the school system in which he or she is enrolled.

Approximately two-thirds of all Indian children (urban and rural) receive services from the IEA. In urban areas program expenditures are approximately $100 per student.[11]

Although levels of expenditures have increased steadily the IEA has not been fully funded. This is because Congress has felt that the program overlaps other educational efforts which serve Indians, namely the Johnson-O'Malley Act and the BIA educational program. While the USOE maintains that no duplication exists, the issue remains controversial. However, the Johnson-O'Malley Act and the BIA programs serve reservation Indians.

The Indian Education Act is the only federal Indian program for which urban Indians are eligible. Thus, the fact that Congress has limited funding for the IEA has meant that urban Indians have borne the brunt of the effect of this decision.

In spite of total expenditures of nearly $100 million between 1972-1975, there has been very little evaluation of the effectiveness of this program in terms of increasing educational achievement or other possible measures of program benefit.

This lack of evaluation has been rationalized by the USOE as follows:

Attempts to evaluate IEA projects on a nationwide basis continue to be hampered by:
a.   the individuality of the funded projects, making evaluative criteria unclear;
b.   the inability to identify efficient unbiased outcome measures which can be administered by agencies external to the projects;
c.   the absence of methods of standardized terminology and uniform descriptions of project processes;
d.   the inability of federal staff to agree upon the purpose of evaluation and to generate a priority structure to their policy questions.[12]

Standardized tests given as part of a national study of equality of educational opportunity (Coleman Report) have shown that differences in achievement (as measured by grade level equivalents) between Indian and white students ranged on the various tests from 1.7 to 2.1 years for sixth grade students, and from 2.7 to 4.0 years for twelfth grade students.[13]

In two urban school districts served by the Indian Education Act, reading scores during 1974-1975 advanced from 0.8 year in one district to 1.6 years in the other.[14]

A number of school districts served by the program have documented declines in absenteeism of 20-25 percent for the 1973-1975 period.

One factor possibly contributing to improving attendance rates might be an increasing correlation between the school program and actual pupil needs and interests. Another possible contributing factor could be the degree of parental interest and involvement in both program planning and operation, which is reflected favorably in both pupil attitudes and improved attendance.

The National Study of American Indian Education

The National Study of American Indian Education was undertaken by Dr. Robert Havighurst and his colleagues. Field research was carried out on several reservations and in the cities of Los Angeles, Chicago, Minneapolis, and Baltimore. Such topics as the mental ability of Indian children, the mental health of Indian youth, school curriculum, and postsecondary education for Indians were considered.

Part of the research focused on the attitudes of Indian parents and children toward the schools that the latter attend. According to the survey, most Indians indicate that the schools in which their children are enrolled are adequate or good. The majority also have some complaints, but, at most, only one in five students and parents had serious negative comments. However, Indian students surveyed had minimal knowledge of educational alternatives; few knew much about other schools or possible variants to the kind of curriculum, teachers, and school programs that exist at the school they attend.

Parents would probably be more critical if they had wider experience with educational institutions. When interviewed, many exhibited little familiarity with even the schools their own children attend. This is understandable given the difficult social and economic conditions in many urban and rural Indian communities. However, most Indian parents, given this limited experience with schools, have almost no basis for critically evaluating the educational institutions in which their children are enrolled. As Indian parents become more involved in educational activities, their increasing sophistication is likely to result in a more critical stance.[15]

Although most students and parents approved of their schools, there were a number of significant exceptions. The most negative comments tended to come from Indians and Indian communities that have the greatest interaction with white urban communities and where Indian students were a minority of the total enrollment.

Alternative Schools

One response to the inadequacies of public schooling has been the creation of private alternative schools. In the 1960s hundreds of alternative schools were begun throughout the United States. Many of these schools emphasized total freedom for individual students.[16] Such "free schools" as they were frequently labeled, rejected the allegedly rigid bureaucratic structure of traditional institutions and attempted to establish a totally different kind of educational curriculum and environment. Other alternative schools, however, maintained an emphasis on academic skills and formal classroom instruction. The common underlying element of these various experiments was dissatisfaction with the education offered by public schools. Although the mortality rate was high, some of these schools maintain viable educational programs and continue operating today.[17]

There are at least eleven Indian alternative or "survival" schools in the country. Evaluating the merits of alternative schools is difficult because one lacks the necessary information to compare these schools with public institutions. It would be useful, for example, to know the percentage of graduates who enter college from alternative and traditional schools. Among those native Americans not entering a post-secondary school, it would be informative to know what kinds of jobs or other kinds of endeavors people obtain upon graduation from public as well as alternative schools. A survey of students and parents in both types of schools regarding their degree of satisfaction with the educational program would provide another comparative yardstick. There is clearly a need for research of this kind that would allow for a more solid comparison between public and alternative schools.[18]

One weakness of alternative schools for Indians relates to science courses. Most of these schools lack funds for the quantity and quality of scientific equipment and laboratory facilities generally found in public schools.

The Dorothy Le Page Indian Community School, Milwaukee, Wisconsin—A Case Study

The school was started in the fall of 1970 by three Indian mothers and seven students in a living room. The number of Indian pupils grew rapidly and the school obtained the use of a basement in one of the local churches. Shortly thereafter, the American Indian Movement (a militant native American organization) obtained control of an abandoned Coast Guard station and allotted space in it to the school.[19]

The philosophy of the school is to provide an academically oriented quality education with an "Indianess core." The school has a strong math and reading program with a major focus on remedial work. In addition, there is emphasis on Indian languages. Persons from the reservations are used as visiting instructors and five different Indian languages are taught.

The school has 102 students attending grades kindergarten through twelfth. The number of teachers at the school is nine. Two of them are part-time and six are native American. The school receives funds from the following sources:[20]

Indian Education Act	$135,000
Department of Agriculture Food Program	17,200
Work Incentive Program	9,208
Donations	724
Total	$161,482

The level of expenditures is $1,600 per student, which is about double the national average for the public schools.

One of the major problems is staff turnover, partly because there are better paying and more secure jobs elsewhere. Moreover, it is difficult to find qualified Indians to teach some subjects.

An interesting educational program has been developed in Chicago by the Native American Committee, Inc. The program is affiliated with Antioch College which awards a B.A. upon completion. The program is intended to provide management training for Indians working in the administration of native American programs. Credit is given for past work experience, and all courses are graded on a pass/fail basis. A major administrative project must be completed before graduation. The core faculty are all Indian, and non-Indian teachers cannot become permanent faculty members or have any responsibility for making program policy decisions. In 1977, there was one graduate and in 1978 there are expected to be three to four additional graduates. While the program is small, it is helping to provide qualified Indian administrators for the many native American programs in Chicago.[21]

Urban Indian Education in Minneapolis—A Case Study

The Minneapolis public school system includes sixty-six elementary schools, fifteen junior high schools, and eleven senior high schools. In the fall of 1973, there were 2,545 native American students (identified by a sight count), who comprised 24.4 percent of the minority student population and 4.3 percent of all students.[22] (Many native Americans believe that the sight-count method of enumeration results in a substantial undercounting of Indian pupils.)

Table 6-7 indicates the distribution of students by grade level. The figures imply a high attrition rate among American Indian students since the proportion of students who are Indian is one-half as great in the upper as compared to the lower grades.

The number of Indian students showed wide variance from school to school.

Table 6-7

Student Distribution by Grade Level—Minneapolis Public Schools, October 1973

Grade Level	Total Number of Students	Number of Native American Students	Percentage of Native American Students
Prekindergarten	81	15	18.52
Kindergarten—am	2,452	126	5.14
Kindergarten—pm	1,882	93	4.94
1	3,707	211	5.69
2	3,236	202	6.24
3	3,337	198	5.93
4	3,482	189	5.43
5	3,531	191	5.41
6	3,951	221	5.59
Ungraded	2,803	74	2.64
Special	757	20	2.64
Total	29,219	1,540	5.27
7	4,228	201	4.75
8	4,361	176	4.04
9	4,686	169	3.61
Ungraded	234	8	3.42
Special	454	56	12.33
Total	13,963	610	4.37
10	5,028	167	3.32
11	4,495	100	2.22
12	4,002	54	1.35
Ungraded	447	16	3.58
Special	573	13	2.27
Adult	1,106	45	4.07
Total	15,651	395	2.52
Grand Total	58,833	2,545	4.33

Source: Minnesota Advisory Committee to the U.S. Commission on Civil Rights, *Bridging the Gap: The Twin Cities' Native American Community* (January 1975), mimeographed, p. 36.

For instance, nine of the sixty-six elementary schools had native American enrollment of at least 10 percent of the student body. Among the junior highs one had a student body that was one-third Indian and two other junior high schools were one-tenth Indian. Among the two senior high schools, one had a 10 percent Indian enrollment while the proportion in the other was almost 6 percent.[23]

The high school dropout rate among American Indians in Minneapolis is about 65 percent compared to 15 percent for all students.

To reduce the high Indian dropout rate, the Minneapolis public schools initiated the Student Support Program during the 1971-1972 school term. Funded by the U.S. Office of Education, the program's allocation for 1974 was $540,131.[24] It has three components: academic, work experience, and social support services. As of January 1974, resources were focused on the three secondary schools with the highest enrollments of native American students.

A recent evaluation indicates that the dropout rate in the target schools has not decreased appreciably since the program's inception and that the program has had no effect on school attendance. One positive result of this effort is that it succeeded, for the first time, in bringing Indian professionals into the school system—about nineteen in all.[25]

The number of native American personnel employed by the Minneapolis school district does not reflect the percentage of native American students enrolled. In November 1974, approximately 1.4 percent of the school employees were Indian. Of the thirty-two hundred teachers employed as of January 1974, fifteen or 0.5 percent were native American. Only two were elementary school teachers, although 60.5 percent of all native American students were enrolled in the elementary schools.[26]

To obtain more Indian professionals, the school district has sponsored the Career Opportunity Program. This effort has had limited success in recruiting native American professionals. Federally funded under the Education Professions Development Act, the program trains inner city residents for careers in education and social work. Participants are employed as salaried teachers' aides while attending college. Tuition, books, and transportation costs are assumed by the program. In 1973-1974 there were ninety participants, ten of whom were native Americans.[27]

One aspect of the Indian educational experience in Minneapolis that many would find disturbing is the disproportionate number of Indian students placed in special education classes (see table 6-7). The statistics indicate that 10.9 percent of all native American students are in special education classes.

Persons with expertise in the area of special education maintain that 3 percent of any given population can be expected to be mentally handicapped in some way,[28] and thus need special education services. Moreover, they feel that among all races, there is a random distribution of qualities, talents, and handicaps.[29] Based on these two assumptions, no racial group should have *significantly* more or less than 3 percent of the population enrolled in special education classes, and no racial group's participation in special education should be significantly different from that group's enrollment in the total school population.

Alternative and Supplementary Education Programs

Both supplementary and alternative education programs for Indian children have been developed in Minneapolis.

One important program is the Indian Upward Bound Program which originated in 1968 as a coordinated effort between the Indian community, the Minneapolis public schools, and the University of Minnesota. The program is funded through a grant from the U.S. Office of Education.

The program is staffed by a director, a cultural arts instructor, a guidance counselor, four teachers' aides, and two secretaries. The principal governing body is an Indian board of directors, of whom approximately 60 percent are parents of children enrolled in the program. For the 1973-1974 school term, 122 students from the seventh, eighth, ninth, and tenth grades participated in the program. These students were provided counseling and tutoring services in local churches and junior high schools. Reading and mathematics were stressed and instruction was offered at the centers for three hours a day.

School attendance for the students participating in Upward Bound has improved about 30 percent and verbal and mathematics achievement levels have increased substantially. Apparently the program has succeeded in reducing the dropout rate as those who graduated in 1973 lost only one-third of their classmates. However, an additional one-third were still in school.[30]

The Heart of the Earth Survival School was established as an alternative school in 1971 and enrolls about 110 students with a staff of ten. The school receives $100,000 in federal funds from the Office of Indian Education.[31] Some private foundations and church groups also provide funds to the school.

The Heart of the Earth school has a strong Indian studies component in its curriculum. Through courses in social studies, culture, and art, as well as those which Heart of the Earth pupils attend at other educational institutions, students are offered instruction in various aspects of Indian culture.

Although school officials claim that attendance and dropout rates are more favorable in comparison to those for Indians in the public schools, little data is available to support these contentions. The school is not accredited by the state of Minnesota, but apparently this has not prevented some graduates from gaining college entrance.

The Kenny Rehabilitation Institute administered the Wide Range Achievement Test to forty-one students attending Heart of the Earth Survival School. The results are shown in table 6-8.

If these gains in achievement levels persist, and can be generalized to the entire Indian student population attending this school, it implies that the institution's methods of instruction are highly effective and should be emulated elsewhere.

Curriculum

Indian culture courses are concentrated in the Minneapolis public schools with the highest Indian enrollments. A task force on ethnic studies is also assisting in

Table 6-8
Wide Range Achievement Test Scores for Children Attending Heart of the Earth Survival School

Test	1972 Grade Level Achievement	1973 Grade Level Achievement
Reading	4.94	7.01
Spelling	4.60	5.52
Arithmetic	4.52	6.30

Source: Minnesota Advisory Committee to the U.S. Commission on Civil Rights, *Bridging the Gap: The Twin Cities' Native American Community* (January 1975), mimeographed, p. 54.

curriculum development. It has developed a variety of materials for use at various grade levels dealing with topics in Indian studies. These materials have been integrated into the regular social studies curriculum. They have also been used to develop some supplementary units which are supportive of special programs in Indian studies. Some of the Indian culture units prepared by the Task Force include: Indian Games; Indian Music; Indian Legends; American Indian Art Slides; Indian Poetry; Contemporary Indian Short Stories; The First Americans, Yesterday and Today; Contacts on the Frontier; Modern Issues: The American Indians; and American Indian Recipes.

Elementary school pupils use "multi-media unit/pacs" which focus on important Minnesota tribes, other U.S. tribes, and Latin American groups. The interactions between the various tribes are considered.

Indian studies courses are offered at the senior high school level and in one school may be used as a substitute for English or social studies credit.

The Indian Education Act provides about $.25 million dollars in funds for Minneapolis Indians.[32] Fifty-three persons are employed including a project administrator, staff developer, coordinator of social work services, thirty-five social worker aides, three Indian student advocates, ten Indian student tutors, and two clerical workers.[33] About two thousand Indians, or 80 percent of the student population, are served.

By law, Title I of the Elementary and Secondary Education Act (ESEA) of 1965 provides financial assistance to local educational agencies for the education of low-income families. Minneapolis public schools receive about $4 million annually from this program. This money has been used to improve education for students in thirty-eight schools and other locations designated as ESEA I target area facilities. Within this area roughly twenty-two thousand pupils are served, of whom 8.5 percent were native Americans. Based upon these figures, 85.7 percent of all native American students were enrolled in ESEA I target area schools.[34]

Summary

Indian pupils must adjust to a very different school environment in the cities as compared to the reservation schools or other rural community schools. They are more likely to comprise a small proportion of total enrollment in the city and to study a curriculum wholly unrelated to their cultural background. Native American students in cities may face prejudice and hostility from their fellow students, and teachers in metropolitan areas are generally unfamiliar with the problems of the urban Indian.

These and other factors tend to cause poor achievement levels among native American students as well as high dropout rates. The latter occurs in spite of substantial evidence that urban Indian economic status is enhanced by completing secondary school.

The U.S. Office of Education operates a number of programs which deliver services to both rural and urban Indians. The impact of these programs is largely unknown. This is partly because USOE is not sure how many Indians are really served by its programs, and, in addition, appropriate evaluation measures have not been developed.

Alternative schools have been established in a number of Indian communities. The performance of these schools vis-à-vis the public schools should be carefully studied. At present, little research has been done on this issue. However, alternative schools do need greater funding for laboratories and scientific equipment.

Notes

1. The most comprehensive survey of educational institutions operated by the Bureau of Indian Affairs on behalf of reservation Indians is, U.S. Congress, Senate Committee on Labor and Public Welfare, Special Subcommittee on Indian Education, *Indian Education: A National Tragedy—A National Challenge* (Washington, D.C., 1969), Report No. 91-501, 91st Congress, 1 session.

2. John S. Morris, "Education and the Urban Indian," in Vine Deloria, ed., *Indian Education Confronts the Seventies, Volume 5, Future Concerns* (Oglala, South Dakota: American Indian Resource Associates, 1974), p. 147.

3. John Peck, "Education of Urban Indians: Lumbee Indians in Baltimore," in *The National Study of American Indian Education* (1969) mimeographed, pp. 3-5; Robert J. Havighurst, "Indians and Their Educations in Los Angeles" (1970), p. 7; Estelle Fuchs and Robert Havighurst, *To Live on This Earth: American Indian Education* (Garden City, New York: Doubleday, 1972), pp. 110-111.

4. Morris, "Education and the Urban Indian," p. 154.

5. Patrick Petit and Murray Wax, "Indian Education in Eastern Oklahoma" (U.S. Office of Education); Report of Research, part 3 (January 1969).

6. Arthur Harkins, et al., "Junior High School Children in Minneapolis: A Study of One Problem School" (Minneapolis, Minnesota: University of Minnesota Training Center for Community Programs, July 1970), p. 53. Moreover, a national survey indicated that 70 percent of classroom teachers for Indian children have had no parental contact.

7. Fuchs and Havighurst, *To Live on This Earth,* pp. 115-116.

8. Task Force Five on Indian Education, *Final Report to the American Indian Policy Review Commission* (Washington, D.C.: U.S. Government Printing Office, 1976), p. 93.

9. Ibid., p. 105. It is estimated that between one-half of 1 percent and 2 percent of all Indian children are taught by native American teachers.

10. "The Indian Education Act of 1972," *Indian Educational Record of Oklahoma* 3, no. 1 (1977):3-7.

11. U.S. Office of Education, Office of Indian Education, *The Third Annual Report to the Congress of the United States* (Washington, D.C.: U.S. Government Printing Office, 1976), pp. 11-4-III-5.

12. Ibid., pp. 1-3.

13. Source U.S. Office of Education, "Dynamics of Achievement: A Study of Differential Growth of Achievement Over Time," Technical Note no. 53, Equal Educational Opportunity Study (Washington, D.C., 1966), mimeographed, table 3. The Indians taking these achievement tests were enrolled in public schools and generally lived in urban areas.

14. U.S. Office of Education, *The Third Annual Report,* p. III-27.

15. Fuchs and Havighurst, *To Live on This Earth,* p. 181.

16. See for example, A.S. Neill, *Summerhill: A Radical Approach to Child Rearing* (New York: Hart Publishing Co., 1960); John Holt, *How Children Fail* (New York: Dell Publishing Co., 1964); Jonathan Kozol, *Death at an Early Age* (Boston: Houghton Mifflin Co., 1967); Jonathan Kozol, *Free Schools* (Boston: Houghton Mifflin Co., 1972).

17. Allen Graubard, "The Free School Movement," *Harvard Educational Review* (August 1972).

18. In an unpublished manuscript, *Open Schools* (1973) Lee Joiner reported the results of a two-year study of alternative schools in Minneapolis: The basic findings were that fourth, fifth, and sixth graders attending alternative schools became more alienated and had lower academic achievement than public school students while just the opposite pattern was uncovered for secondary school students. See Wilbur B. Brookover and Edsel Eridsson, *Sociology of Education* (Homewood, Illinois: Dorsey Press, 1975), p. 351.

19. Task Force Five, *Final Report,* p. 357.

20. Ibid.

21. Interview with Fay Smith, Native American Educational Committee, Inc. (August 1977).

22. Minneapolis Public Schools, Special School District No. 1, Planning and Support Services, *1973-1974 Pupil-Personnel Sight Count* (October 16, 1973).

23. Minnesota Advisory Commission on Civil Rights, *Bridging the Gap: The Twin Cities' Native American Community* (January, 1975), mimeographed, p. 35.

24. Minneapolis Public Schools, "Planning, Development, and Federal Programs—Native American Participation in Federally Funded Programs" (1973-1974).

25. American Institutes for Research, "Title VIII, Student Support Program, Minneapolis Public Schools, Evaluation Report, 1972-1973" (July 1973), p. 9.

26. Minneapolis Public Schools, Special School District No. 1, *1973-1974 Pupil-Personnel Sight Count.*

27. Minnesota Advisory Commission on Civil Rights, *Bridging the Gap,* p. 43.

28. See D. Wechsler, *The Measurement and Appraisal of Adult Intelligence,* 4th ed. (Baltimore: Williams and Wilkins, 1958); and L.M. Terman and M.A. Merill, *Stanford Binet Intelligence Scale* (Boston: Houghton Mifflin Co., 1960).

29. The use of this assumption can be seen, for instance, in Larry P. Versus Riles, 343 F. Supp. 1306 (N.D. Cal. 1972); see also, "Legal Implication of the Use of Standardized Ability Tests in Employment and Education," *Columbia Law Review* 68 (1968):691 and 695.

30. Minnesota Advisory Commission on Civil Rights, *Bridging the Gap,* pp. 50-51.

31. Ibid., p. 52.

32. Minneapolis Public Schools, "Federal Funding—Benefits to Native American Students" (January 1974).

33. Paul Day, "Program and Services to Indian Students in Minneapolis Public Schools" (January 1974).

34. Minneapolis Public Schools, Special School District No. 1, *1973-1974 Pupil-Personnel Sight Count,* pp. 109-111.

7 Urban Indian Institutions

One of the most important Indian ethnic institutions in urban areas has been the Indian bar. In hundreds of towns and cities, Indians congregate in particular places to drink. There is considerable social animation and interaction in Indian bars. People are loud and overtly friendly to both acquaintances and strangers alike as they go from table to table and bar to bar. Gangs develop readily for such crimes as robbing drunks and engaging in prostitution. Many Indians who become deeply enmeshed in the bar culture end up on skid row and ultimately in jail.[1]

The bar crowd and attendant socializing become very important to urban Indians because for many of them it is the only recreational activity in which they can engage and feel accepted. Moreover, for newly arrived migrants it serves as a place to meet old friends from the reservation as well as to make new friends. However, these cliques generally adapt a lifestyle that reduces the likelihood of a successful adjustment to city life. Indians generally have a heritage of opposition to the dominant white culture. This becomes stronger if they adopt the activity pattern of skid row whites, and experience the police harassment of all skid row inhabitants while attempting to adjust to urban society. As a result, the Indian who lives on skid row usually leaves there within a year or two and either returns to the reservation or reduces his rate of drinking and becomes a more stable member of urban society. For the younger Indian this is a highly mobile period in his life. He often obtains temporary employment and moves frequently back and forth from the reservation to the city.

White social service organizations are generally unsympathetic to the problems of skid row inhabitants but may be quite concerned with the problems of Indian migrants to the city and the conditions of local Indians generally. In response to this concern, service-oriented religious organizations have often established an Indian center. For example, in Los Angeles, the Society of Friends (the Quaker church) developed the first Indian organization. This was later supported by local civic clubs and other churches. The initial focus of the center was social welfare and the organization engaged in such activities as job and family counseling and the distribution of donated food and clothing. In time, however, Indians who had successfully adjusted to urban life gradually obtained control of the center and shifted the emphasis away from social assistance. They developed a small, separate organization for the delivery of welfare services, but the focus changed toward athletics, powwows, and an actors' workshop to train people for the movie industry. A second Indian center

107

was established by another Christian church organization to serve the welfare needs of the newly arrived migrant Indians.[2]

The initial stage in the development of urban Indian ethnic institutions is evidenced by the dominance of the bar culture. This situation exists in many small towns and cities, in both Canada and the western United States. However, most of the urban areas with several thousand Indians have developed Indian centers and related Indian organizations. There appears to be some lag in the development of centers and other organizations if the Indians come from reservations in the immediate region. For example, most urban migrants to Dallas come from the various reservations and Indian land areas in Oklahoma. An Indian center was not established until 1969 and even today there are far fewer Indian organizations in Dallas than other cities with comparable levels of Indian population.

In the situation where there is a relatively large urban Indian population, the newly arrived migrant can ask friends and relatives in the city for assistance. These developing friendship networks become institutions that carry on many of the same functions as an Indian bar or an Indian center, and thus serve as an alternative means of entry into urban life. These networks are *second stage institutions* that promote and facilitate the migration of Indians to cities. They operate without the negative aspects of the bar culture and without the alleged paternalism of white church agencies.

There is usually a decrease in the number of predominantly Indian bars during the second stage of development of Indian institutions because other organizations provide for the social and educational needs of most new migrants. Thus, Indian centers and friends and relatives provide the bulk of assistance to newcomers. Moreover, many Indians move away from the transient skid row area to more stable residential neighborhoods, and, in addition, people tend to shift their drinking to homes and private parties. Thus, Los Angeles, a city with some 45,000-60,000 Indians, has only three predominantly Indian bars. Dallas has 16,000-20,000 Indians and only one predominantly Indian bar. These cities are in a relatively mature stage of Indian ethnic institutionalization.

Ablon found that individual migrants to the San Francisco Bay area would typically go through an initial seeking-out period, usually including an approach to an Indian center, and subsequently would engage in more diverse social interactions forming friendships on the job, in the neighborhood, or at church.[3] Family life became more time consuming as the size of an individual's family grew, and most families attended only the major Indian events, such as a Christmas party, an annual picnic, a dance, or a powwow. The formal institutions were used more by new migrants who needed security in a new environment and the opportunity to socially interact with others in a similar situation. The most important sources of friends and other social contacts were: (1) relatives and friends from the reservation; (2) Indian centers and related organizations; (3) housing projects, neighborhoods, stores, and public places; and

(4) places of employment. The social interactions increased over time in all four of these contexts. The amount of time spent in church groups, government-sponsored events or programs, and bars either remained about the same or declined.

The third stage in the development of urban Indian institutions occurs when the organizations include a broad range of common interest associations such as Indian athletic leagues, Indian Christian churches, powwow clubs, and political organizations. In the third stage the Indians develop their own unique ethnic institutions, often associated with promoting a positive image of the Indian, as opposed to attempting to solve the socioeconomic problems of Indians as they are perceived to exist by non-Indians. At this stage institutions are dominated by Indian staffs, who are quite critical of the earlier assistance efforts of non-Indians because of the alleged paternalistic style in which services were delivered.

The first Indians to be associated with all native institutions are usually the most acculturated. They often develop policies that are pro-white and assimilationist. For example, there were several urban clubs of whites and acculturated Indians in the 1920s: Chicago's Grand Council Fire of the American Indians, Seattle's National Society of Indian Women, and four clubs in Los Angeles—American Indian Progressive Association, the Indian Women's Club, the Wigwam Club for Native Dancing, and the War Paint Club for Indians in the movie industry.[4]

Increased migration has affected these organizations because of the changing relationship between acculturated and unacculturated persons. As indicated above, the institution may have been started by whites with acculturated Indians subsequently becoming dominant; or it may have been established by acculturated Indians. However, increased migration of less acculturated Indians has an impact on these organizations. Over time, as the latter increase their participation in the organizations, they try to redirect the institutions, to their ends, as opposed to the interests of whites or acculturated Indians. Most Indian institutions, however, are at least partly controlled by acculturated Indians because more recent migrants frequently lack the administrative skills to successfully operate the institution and raise the funds to sustain operations.

The Indian Center

There is no question that Indian centers throughout the United States have provided vital services to urban Indians including personal and financial counseling, providing referral to other organizations (both Indian and non-Indian) primarily for social services, and serving as a location for social and athletic events.

Moreover, Indian centers have assumed the role of advocate for Indian persons and organizations. By serving as the primary communication link between Indian people and the various levels of government in a metropolitan area, Indian centers are often able to obtain an increase in services for Indian individuals and families.[5]

For newly arrived urban Indians, the centers' first function is to provide emergency care. This care may range from provision of food and clothing to finding housing and tracking down relatives who can assist the newcomer.

Although there is no "typical" Indian center, the organization formed in Lincoln, Nebraska has a set of goals and purposes which are generally found elsewhere. The center was formed in June 1969 to encourage "integration of the city's 1,440 American Indian residents, regardless of time honored tribal differences."[6] The center's purposes are as follows:[7]

1. To establish a continuing program which will help the American Indian help himself.
2. To help the American Indian adapt to urban life.
3. To make the American Indian aware of the available services in education, employment, housing, hospitalization, alcohol treatment and rehabilitation, credit union financing and membership.
4. To organize and create arts and crafts industries and develop job opportunities through the center.
5. To help in any way possible the American Indian both on and off the reservation.
6. To help combat juvenile delinquency among American Indians.
7. To encourage sports programs among American Indians such as, but not limited to, baseball, football, track, and boxing.
8. To help eliminate prejudice and discrimination.
9. To defend human rights of the American Indian, guaranteed by law.

Membership in the center is not limited to American Indians but the members of the board of directors must be Indian. In addition, the board must be representative of all tribes in the organization. These include the Pottawatomie, Sioux, Winnebago, Cherokee, and Lumbee.[8]

Perhaps the most important contribution of the urban centers to the Indian living in cities has been a psychological one. Having left the Indian community, and often their families, migrant Indians are victims of isolation and loneliness. They have developed these centers to ameliorate such problems and to provide a place where they can join together in social gatherings that substitute for the personal security of the reservation. Some of these centers have evolved from very small groups organized for recreational purposes into diverse operations with programs in the areas of employment assistance, defense of tenants' rights, entertainment, and welfare assistance.[9]

Indian Center Problems

One of the principal problems Indian centers have faced is a lack of sustained funding. Because urban Indians have low incomes, it is difficult for many to make a substantial financial contribution to the centers. As a result much of the funding has come from church organizations, the United Givers Fund, and other charitable organizations, and in the mid and late 1960s, from the Office of Economic Opportunity (OEO) programs. Because of lack of funding, many persons worked in these centers as volunteers. They served and continue to serve out of a feeling of responsibility to the Indian community. However, there was considerable turnover of volunteers who often lacked technical expertise in their areas of center responsibility.

The financing situation for Indian centers brightened with the passage of the Native Americans Program Act of 1974. The major purpose of this legislation is "to provide technical assistance, training, and financial support to help native Americans achieve economic and social independence by enabling them to identify their own needs; establish their own priorities; conduct their own programs to meet those needs; and control the institutions and programs that affect their daily lives."[10]

During 1977 the Office of Native American Programs (ONAP) funded sixty urban Indian centers with an expenditure of $5 million. The minimum grant is $40,000 and the maximum grant is $200,000. The city in which the center is established must have at least thirty thousand residents and there must be at least one thousand Indians residing in the city. The level of the grant (up to the maximum) is $42 per urban Indian.[11]

In most cases this funding has served as "seed" money for additional grants. An official with the ONAP in Washington told the author that most centers are able to generate two to three times as much additonal funding from other agencies as compared to the original ONAP grant.

As indicated above, prior to ONAP funding, most Indian centers had chronic financial problems. For example, the Lincoln, Nebraska Indian Center originally received most of its funds from various religious organizations including the City Mission, The Reconciliation Task for Disciples of Christ, and the Nebraska Conference of the United Methodist Church. Although the center struggled to remain independent of these organizations, this was not really possible before federal funds were obtained from ONAP.

One of the factors that has limited the ability of the Indian center to obtain adequate services for Indians from programs for the overall population, as well as to obtain federal grants for its own programs, has been the lack of adequate statistics regarding the population of urban Indian communities. With funding levels often based on population size, lack of accurate information in this regard has likely resulted in lower allocations to the urban Indian community than would have occurred if more accurate statistics were available. This is because existing information probably understates the actual Indian population in most cities. Moreover, data is lacking regarding the need within the community for such items as health services. The importance of accurate data regarding the size and socioeconomic status of the urban Indian community cannot be overemphasized. Such information is a vital first step in the planning and delivery of services to urban Indians.

Another major problem affecting the stability and effectiveness of Indian centers is the occurrence of factionalism and infighting. While some may deem it inappropriate to generalize, it appears that often Indians are quite competitive among other native Americans while passive or noncompetitive when dealing with non-Indians. Some of this factionalism is based on personal jealousy and tribal differences; in other cases it seems related to competition for the few relatively well-paying jobs which are available through federally funded Indian center programs. However, regardless of the cause, infighting has limited center operations and retarded the development of a Pan-Indian movement. This problem can best be illustrated by several examples.

During the 1960s the program and staff of the Chicago Indian Center had grown steadily. Late in 1967, the center bought a Masonic temple at 1630 West Wilson Avenue, in the heart of the Chicago Indian community. The purchase of such a large building gave a greater sense of permanence to the center and also gave impetus to the hiring of additional staff for maintenance and an expanded program. By 1970 there were more than twenty full and part-time employees.[12] However, in 1971, shortly after the death of the executive director, Mr. Robert Rietz, two factions developed among the board of directors and the staff. One faction left the center and started a new group called the Native American Committee (NAC). The Native American Committee had been a group meeting at the center before the split. It originated in support of the Indians who took over Alcatraz Island in 1969.[13]

At the time of the schism and for some time thereafter, the Indian center had a full program including legal assistance services, cultural and recreational programs, social services including individual and family counseling, and a day camp and explorers program for children.

However, the Native American Committee, which now receives $400,000 annually in federal funds,[14] began duplicating many of the center's activities, and in addition, developed an alternative education center. The latter was designed for children who were not adjusting well in the public schools. Moreover, NAC presently operates an adult education program, a mental health program, and an arts and crafts shop.[15]

The Indian center could not meet the competition of NAC partly because the former had never sought or wanted federal funding. Local institutions were reluctant to fund an organization that would provide services similar to those provided by NAC, which is federally funded. The Community Chest which had financially supported the Indian center for many years withdrew its support when it objected to the way in which the center's accounts and bookkeeping were being handled. At present, the center is on the verge of bankruptcy. It is over $75,000-$100,000 in debt,[16] has no director, only two or three staff, and has almost no viable programs. Should federal funding for NAC decline, Indians in Chicago may be without any major Indian-run organization for basic social services.

In Dallas, the American Indian Center was founded in 1969 and a faction within the organization departed and formed their own organization, the Dallas Inter-Tribal Center and Clinic in July 1971. However, these two centers do not compete with each other but instead offer complementary programs. The Inter-Tribal Center operates a free clinic, the CETA program, and an outpatient alcoholism program. The American Indian Center operates a preschool program with $330,000 grant from the Office of Indian Education, a social services program, and a residential treatment program for alcoholics. A number of inpatients are referred from the outpatient program of the Inter-Tribal Center.[17]

In Baltimore, the American Indian Study Center was begun in August 1968, so that "Indian culture, Indian life, history and craft could be shared with one another," and in which there could be "an emphasis upon establishing and maintaining a proper image of the American Indian in the interest of all peoples concerned."[18] The center was initially supported by grants from the Community Action Agency (antipoverty) Program and a private organization interested in promoting knowledge of Indian culture.[19]

The center's programs remained limited until 1974-1975 when federal support was received for three major programs: an ONAP grant which provided core funding for the center, a CETA grant for job training, and an alcoholism grant from the National Institute for Alcoholism and Drug Abuse.

At about this time factionalism erupted based on personal differences and disputes as to who was to be employed in the federally funded programs. The director was accused of irregularities in the handling of funds and of receiving a full-time salary when he had another full-time position. In the ensuing hiatus, the Department of Labor removed the CETA grant from the center,[20] and ONAP withdrew core funding support.[21] The insurgent faction ousted the executive director and his supporters, but in a sense had a hollow victory because of the precarious state of the center's financial situation and limited programs.

Aside from factionalism and infighting, Indian centers face considerable competition from other Indian organizations for receipt of federal grants. There are twelve major Indian organizations in Los Angeles, twenty-four in Minneapolis, and eleven in Chicago.[22] Many of these organizations offer services that duplicate those being provided by other groups, particularly in the areas of social services and alcoholism. From the standpoint of efficiency it would make more sense to have one or two organizations developing expertise and services of a particular type rather than a multiplicity of organizations continually trying to outdo each other.

The Los Angeles Indian Center (AIC) recently lost a $1 million CETA grant to another Indian organization called the Tribal American Corporation. One of the reasons for the loss of funding was that while the program was at AIC the proportion of enrollees completing training was only 42 percent.[23] Moreover, the Tribal American Corporation, which has considerable experience in the consulting field and in the operation of day care and preschool programs, has had a remarkable degree of stability among Indian organizations. Tribal American has no internal squabbles and has stayed out of the political infighting that frequently occurs between Indian organizations.[24]

One way to make the process of federal assistance more efficient would be to give grants to Indian organizations for a period of several years. When grants must be renewed each year much effort goes into writing grant proposals instead of improving the quality of service. If funding were available for longer periods of time, one could more readily determine whether a particular organization was able to provide satisfactory services and whether the grant should be renewed.

In an ideal situation several urban Indian organizations would agree to work cooperatively instead of competitively. Each organization would specialize in the delivery of those services which it could provide most effectively. A clearing-house would screen various grant proposals and refer them to the organization which seemed most appropriate. The Indian Commission of Los Angeles is supposed to assist Indian organizations in obtaining grants and to exercise a clearinghouse function. However, there is no evidence that it has succeeded in reducing the amount of competition for funds and duplication of effort among Indian organizations.

A final difficulty that plagues Indian centers as well as other Indian organizations is staff turnover and vacancies. In each of five Indian centers recently visited, the position of director was vacant. Other key positions are frequently unfilled. Part of the turnover is related to infighting and factionalism which results in the members of one group either resigning or being fired by the other (dominant) group. Another reason for the turnover and vacancies is that with the upsurge in federal programs for native Americans, Indians who are college trained are in relatively short supply. Thus, the shortage of personnel and the plethora of organizations encourage people to move from one organization to another to obtain the highest salary possible. This behavior, of course, is precisely what one would expect of non-Indians under similar circumstances.

Indian Business Development Associations

Most cities with relatively large Indian populations have only a handful of Indian-owned businesses. For example, in Baltimore there are about thirty

Indian-owned businesses compared to twelve to twenty-five Indian businesses in Chicago and twenty in Minneapolis. Minneapolis businesses include two bars, a printing company, two construction companies, two auto repair concerns, and two arts and crafts stores.[25]

To accelerate the number of Indian-owned businesses the Department of Commerce's Office of Minority Business Enterprise (OMBE) has funded a number of Indian business development organizations that provide technical assistance and help in locating financing as well as marketing research for new and existing businesses.

The fortunes of these organizations have differed greatly. The American Indian Business Association of Chicago recently lost its OMBE grant. The major reason given was that the businesses that were assisted were too small to justify continued federal support of the program. This view seems shortsighted.[26] Few Indians would have the credit availability, personal financial resources, or business experience to initially develop a medium-sized or large business. Since virtually all Indians have no previous business experience, it is more reasonable to expect that initial entrepreneurial efforts would be small.

The most successful business development organization in the country is the United Indian Development Association of Los Angeles (UIDA). Formed in 1970, when only a small handfull of Indian businesses existed in California, the organization makes available free management and technical assistance to more than 450 Indian-owned businesses in that state (primarily in urban areas). In addition to funding from the Office of Minority Business Enterprise, UIDA receives grants and contributions from more than twenty large businesses and institutions in the Los Angeles area.

During 1976-1977, more than seventeen hundred jobs were created within new and existing Indian businesses.[27] Moreover, UIDA personnel helped obtain more than $2.2 million in contracts for Indian businesses throughout California as well as $1.7 million in bank financing for Indian men and women. The combined total of $3.9 million represents an increase of more than $1 million over the 1975-1976 results obtained by the association.

As table 7-1 indicates, UIDA's contribution to the American Indian economy has increased dramatically over the past five years, beginning with a base of only $150,000 in contracts during the 1972-1973 period. Based on its funding level and volume of results, UIDA has received a 12.6:1 return on the funds allocated to the organization by the federal government. In other words, for each dollar funded to UIDA, $12.60 was generated directly back into the economy.[28]

The failure rate for UIDA-assisted businesses has been very low. Only 2 percent of the 450 businesses that have been assisted by the association are no longer in operation.

One of the factors inhibiting urban Indian business development generally is the limited federal funding available to assist Indian business development

Table 7-1

United Indian Development Association—Indicators of Accomplishment

Year	Financing of Indian Business		Contracts Obtained for Indian Business	
	Number	Value	Number	Value
1972-1973	6	$ 150,000	2	$ 50,000
1973-1974	24	550,000	45	500,000
1974-1975	18	800,000	51	1,600,000
1975-1976	24	1,200,000	45	1,700,000
1976-1977	28	1,700,000	151	2,200,000

Source: United Indian Development Association, *Annual Report, 1977* (United Indian Development Association), mimeographed.

organizations. The entire OMBE budget is only $2 million a year.[29] Since Small Business Administration programs have had little impact on the urban Indian community, the need for greater funding through OMBE is clear.

The Indian Financing Act funded by the Bureau of Indian Affairs provides $10 million annually in grants and loans to assist reservation Indians who want to develop or expand a business. Tribes also have access to a $200 million guaranteed loan fund for similar activities. Urban Indians, which total about one-half the total Indian population, receive less than 1 percent of this latter amount.

Religious Social Agencies

In most cities with large Indian populations there are church-affiliated agencies that provide various forms of assistance to Indians, particularly those that have recently arrived from the reservations. Two of the most effective are the Division of Indian Work in Minneapolis, and St. Augustine's Indian Center in Chicago.

The Division of Indian Work of the Greater Minneapolis Council of Churches is a coordinating agency that serves the Indian population through a program of human services supported by the congregations and denominations. The main services are:[30]

1. Counseling Indian families in adjusting to urban life. This involves various activities such as obtaining necessary documents including birth certificates and educational records, employment referral and counseling, tenant-landlord relationships, installment buying, church affiliation, and financial management.
2. Providing emergency services in the areas of health, welfare, housing, and

food, or when necessary, working with other agencies to provide these services.

3. Acquainting Indians with programs and services available to them in the churches and the community.
4. Explaining Indian conditions and programs to churches in the council jurisdiction.
5. Working and relating to social agencies that have demonstrated concerns for Indian people.

The Division of Indian Work recently had its program evaluated by an external task force. The conclusion was as follows:

The Task Force feels that there is absolutely necessary and strategic work being done by the Division of Indian Work which is essential within the Indian community. The effects of the Division of Indian Work in the past 6 years has had substantial impact upon the total community and the Indian people in particular.
"The immediate task includes building upon and extending services already identified by the Division of Indian Work. The credibility of the Division of Indian Work is solid among many Indian people . . . It . . . has been able to encourage and undertake new approaches and programs as well as provide sound support for more established Indian programs.[31]

The budget for the Division of Indian Work is indicated in table 7-2. Considering the fact that there are 15,000-20,000 Indians in the Minneapolis metropolitan area, this organization's limited resources indicate that it can only meet a small fraction of the need.

Although half of the budget is for salaries, this agency is certainly not overstaffed, as there are only two full-time staff personnel, the director and a secretary. The largest non-salary expense is emergency assistance. This is not surprising since it is the heart of the program.

St. Augustine's Indian Center is a social agency of the Episcopal Diocese of Chicago. However, St. Augustine's Center receives no direct financial support from the Diocese, or from the executive council of the Episcopal Church. The center began in 1962 with a budget of $10,500 which by 1970 had grown to $206,000. About 80 percent of the money is or was raised through private donations and, in the recent past, the remaining one-fifth had come from the community action agency.[32] At present the center serves about five hundred families and individuals a month.[33] The center was founded by Father Peter Powell who has continued his association with the center.

The main components of the program are counseling and direct assistance particularly of an emergency nature (see table 7-3). Referral is a relatively minor part of the program. Much of the counseling involves working with chronic alcoholics. With regard to the latter, St. Augustine's has recently expanded its alcoholism services by developing a "drop-in" center which provides food and

118

Table 7-2
Division of Indian Work, Budgets 1976-1979

Income	1976 Budget	1977 Proposed Budget	1978 Proposed Budget	1979 Proposed Budget
Minnesota Council of Churches	$ 9,000	$10,700	$12,000	$ 13,500
Congregations	14,400	10,000	16,000	17,000
Organizations	6,000	4,000	6,000	6,000
Individuals	2,500	2,700	5,000	5,000
Denominations	12,000	8,000	14,000	14,500
Firms and Foundations	2,000	2,000	3,000	3,000
United Way	—	21,000	23,000	25,000
Other Income	200	200	300	300
Greater Minneapolis Council of Churches Allocation	14,335	16,300	19,500	20,800
Total	$60,435	$74,900	$98,800	$105,600

Expense

	1976 Budget	1977 Proposed Budget	1978 Proposed Budget	1979 Proposed Budget
Salaries and Related Expense				
Salaries	$24,000	$28,000	$40,000	$ 42,500
Fringe Benefits	3,300	4,350	6,400	6,900
Staff Expense	1,000	1,050	2,100	1,600
Program Expense				
Supplies and Printing	1,400	1,450	1,550	1,650
Postage	400	500	550	600
Insurance	—	150	200	250
Emergency Assistance	12,200	15,000	18,000	20,000
Student Aid	1,000	3,000	3,000	3,000
Facilities				
Maintenance	1,800	4,000	6,000	6,600
Telephone	1,000	1,100	1,500	1,700
Greater Minneapolis Council of Churches Distributed Expense				
General Office Expense	4,747	5,400	6,500	7,000
Bookkeeping	3,071	3,500	4,200	4,500
Public Relations and Financing	2,985	3,400	4,000	4,200
Central Coordination	3,532	4,000	4,800	5,100
Total	$60,435	$74,900	$98,800	$105,600

Source: Division of Indian Work, Proposed Budget, unpublished tabulation, November 3, 1976.

counseling for about 130 Indians a week.[34] The "drop-in" center, located in the heart of the skid row district, has an all-Indian staff comprising of a director, two counselors, and food preparation personnel. Some clients are referred elsewhere for detoxification. The program is funded through a grant from the Model Cities Program. Non-Indians are occasionally permitted to use the services

Table 7-3
Annual Summary of Services Provided by St. Augustine's Indian Center

Service Components	Participants	Attendance
Counseling		
1. Crisis and short term	963	2771
2. Intensive counseling	439	2651
3. Individual psychotherapy	41	214
Youth Counseling		
1. Tutoring	37	
2. Summer recreational program	76	
Short-Term Assistance		
1. Cash, food, clothing	1248	6680
Referrals		
1. Job	85	96
2. Medical	95	126
3. Legal	30	38
4. Miscellaneous	104	174
Scholarship	7	
Total	1498	13348

Source: St. Augustine's Center for American Indians, *Annual Report 1969-1970* (St. Augustine's Center for American Indians), mimeographed, p. 12.

if the Indians who are there do not object. The program has had few successes thus far, but as long as the individual keeps coming to the "drop-in" center, there is always hope for improvement.

St. Augustine's has sponsored a considerable amount of research regarding the social and economic conditions of its client families and individuals, as well as the problems of Chicago Indians generally. Much of this research is available in book or monograph form or in professional journals.[35]

Many federal agencies (for example, ONAP) will not give grants to St. Augustine's because the board of directors is not elected by the Indian community. Since this organization is a major force among the Indians in Chicago, it appears that existing federal regulations are too inflexible.

Evaluation of Indian Organizations

Probably the most common (and least useful) type of evaluation of Indian organizations has been based on a simple description of the personnel, facilities, and programs that are offered. The information implies that the facilities and services are of some benefit to the population, but no data are presented regarding the effectiveness and, in most cases, the quality of the service. Much of the descriptive material made available for public consumption by Indian organizations falls into this category of evaluation. For example, the brochure published by the Minneapolis Regional Native American Center describes the library, auditorium, audio visual facilities, and gallery. The kinds of programs (social services, education, recreation) are described and the staff and their titles are indicated.[36]

A more useful evaluation focuses on the volume of services provided with perhaps some indication of the proportion of the eligible population that receives services. The data provided in table 7-3 indicating the level of services provided to Indians at St. Augustine's Indian Center would be an appropriate example although no estimates of unmet needs are provided.

A third level of evaluation would consider the *quality* of services provided. One method of ascertaining this would be to interview a representative sample of Indians and ask them which Indian organizations they believe are doing a good job. Another way to determine quality would be to have the Indians rate the effectiveness of the programs operated by particular organizations. The responses might be stratified by length of stay in the city, tribal affiliation, education, income, and age to indicate which segments of the Indian population are dissatisfied with the quality of services provided. Such a survey could become the basis for program modification if required.

The most sophisticated evaluation of organizations and their programs would measure the extent to which the ultimate objective of a program has been achieved. For example, chapter 4 described the establishment of a number of urban Indian health centers. To evaluate them according to this criteria would require a determination as to whether the health of the Indians receiving center services had improved. To carry out such an evaluation, one would have to undertake longitudinal surveys of mortality and morbidity in the population served by the center.[a] This evaluation is most useful because it helps to answer the question, "What difference has the health center really made?" All other levels of evaluation, because of their limited focus, approach this question only indirectly.

Because many urban Indian programs such as the health and alcoholism efforts are so new, such a sophisticated type of evaluation is not presently feasible. However, if the appropriate data collection and information systems were established now, an extensive evaluation could be undertaken within three to five years.

---

[a]Probably the most difficult problem which would have to be faced is that a significant part of the service population is transient and moves back and forth from the reservation to the city while others frequently change addresses within the city. Thus, the number of "dropouts" in a longitudinal health survey would be considerable. Other problems would include obtaining some services from non—Indian organizations and some from reservation sources.

The above comments are also relevant to evaluation of Indian social service programs. Thus, one consideration is whether or not they help make Indian people self-supporting. At this point there is no hard information on this matter—and rigorous evaluation is thus impossible.

At present, most evaluation of urban Indian programs is primitive, primarily because of lack of information and a scarcity of funds for data collection and analysis. Federal grants to Indian agencies should include an evaluation component and increasingly sophisticated evaluations should be made the basis for continued funding.

Summary

The development of Indian institutions and organizations typically goes through three stages: the bar culture, Indian centers and friendship networks, and finally, the development of Pan-Indian ethnic institutions. Most cities with large Indian populations are probably in the second stage of institutional development.

One of the most important Indian organizations in the urban community is the Indian center. Offering a variety of social services, the center can be of great material and psychological comfort for those newly arrived from the reservations. The Native American Program Act of 1974 has made it possible for the federal government to provide core funding. This has partially relieved the financial difficulties facing most centers. Indian center problems include infighting and factionalism, competition for grants with many other organizations, and high staff turnover.

Indian organizations were evaluated on four levels. These are primarily a description of activities, volume and type of services rendered, quality of services provided, and effectiveness of the organization in meeting various goals. It is suggested that objective study of the latter is the most useful means of evaluating program effectiveness.

Notes

1. John Price, "U.S. and Canadian Indian Urban Ethnic Institutions," *Urban Anthropology* 4, no. 1 (1975):40.

2. Ibid., pp. 40-41.

3. Joan Ablon, "Relocated American Indians in the San Francisco Bay Area: Social Interaction and Indian Identity," *Human Organization* 23, no. 4 (1964):296-304.

4. Price, "U.S. and Canadian Indian Urban Ethnic Institutions," p. 43.

5. Task Force Eight on Urban and Rural Non-Reservation Indians, *Final Report to the American Indian Policy Review Commission* (Washington, D.C.: U.S. Government Printing Office, 1976), p. 76.

6. Bess Jenkins, "Lincoln's Indians Join Together to Encourage Integration in City," *Lincoln Journal* (June 8, 1969).

7. Arthur Harkins, Mary Zemyan, and Richard Woods, *Indian Americans in Omaha and Lincoln* (Minnesota: Training Center for Community Programs, University of Minnesota, 1970), p. 35.

8. Jenkins, "Lincoln's Indians."

9. American Indian Policy Review Commission, *Final Report* (Washington, D.C.: U.S. Government Printing Office, 1977), p. 440.

10. U.S. Department of Health, Education, and Welfare, *Office of Native American Programs, 1975* (Washington, D.C.: U.S. Government Printing Office, 1975), DHEW Publication no. (OHD) 75-24000, p. 3.

11. Interview with Ms. Ann Litchfield, Office of Native American Programs (June 1977).

12. Merwyn Gabarino, "The Chicago American Indian Center: Two Decades," in Jack O. Waddell and O. Michael Watson, eds., *American Indian Urbanization* (Lafayette, Indiana: Purdue University, 1973), Institute Monograph Series, no. 4, pp. 81-82.

13. Ibid., p. 83.

14. Interview with Mr. Matt Pilcher, Executive Director, Native American Committee (August 1977).

15. Native American Committee, Inc., "Education-Community-Leadership," mimeographed brochure.

16. Interview with Mr. Robert Huey, Industrial Development Officer, Bureau of Indian Affairs, Chicago Office (August 1977).

17. Interview with an administrative assistant, American Indian Center of Dallas, Texas (August 1977).

18. *American Indian Study Center Newletter* 1, no. 1 (1970).

19. Abraham Makofsky, *Tradition and Change in the Lumbee Indian Community of Baltimore* (Ph.D. dissertation, Catholic University of America, 1971), pp. 190-191.

20. Interview with Ms. Barbara Carroll, Department of Labor (Summer, 1977).

21. Interview with Ms. Ann Litchfield.

22. Indian Clubs and Organizations (Los Angeles, 1977), mimeographed; Division of Indian Work, Metropolitan Resources Directory (Minneapolis, 1977), mimeographed; and Native American Community (Chicago, July 1977), mimeographed.

23. Interview with Harlan Hall, American Indian Center, Inc., Los Angeles (August 1977).

24. Interview with Jim Greycloud, Executive Vice President, Tribal American Corporation (Ausust 1977).

25. Upper Midwest American Indian Center, *American Indian Business Directory* (Minneapolis).

26. Interview with Dr. Robert Snyder, Associate Dean of Business, Roosevelt University, Chicago (August 1977).

27. United Indian Development Association, *Annual Report* (1977), mimeographed.

28. Ibid.

29. Interview with Mr. Joe Vasquez, Office of Minority Business Enterprise, Department of Commerce (June 1977).

30. Division of Indian Work, Greater Minneapolis Council of Churches, *Statement of Purpose* (1976), mimeographed.

31. Minneapolis Indian Center, *Program Task Force Report,* (1976), mimeographed.

32. St. Augustine's Center for American Indians, Inc., *Annual Report, 1969-1970,* mimeographed, p. 3.

33. Interview with Amy Skenandore, Director, St. Augustine's Indian Center (August 1977).

34. Interview with Mr. Richard Elm, Director, St. Augustine's Alcoholism Drop-In Center (August 1977).

35. See for example, Richard Wood and Arthur Harkins, *Indian Americans in Chicago* (Minneapolis, Minnesota: Training Center for Community Programs, November 1968), mimeographed; Profulla Neog, Richard Woods, and Arthur Harkins, *Chicago Indians: The Effects of Urban Migration* (Minneapolis, Minnesota: Training Center for Community Programs, University of Minnesota, January 1970), mimeographed; John White, *Patterns in American Indian Employment* (St. Augustine's Center, 1971); Gerard Littman, "Alcoholism, Illness, and Social Pathology Among American Indians in Transition," *American Journal of Public Health* 60, no. 9 (September 1970):1769-1787.

36. Minneapolis Regional Native American Center, descriptive brochure (undated), mimeographed.

8 Acculturation and Adjustment

American Indians bring a unique cultural heritage to urban society. Most Indians are basically tribally oriented persons who leave the close-knit kinship relationships of a closed reservation community to enter a highly individualistic society. Many fundamental Indian values are not only totally different from those of the dominant culture, but are incompatible with the principles of a competitive capitalistic society.

It is this great value disparity that makes Indians different from most other urban migrants. Indians are generally noncompetitive when among non-Indians, and avoid competitive activities and aggressive action whenever possible. They tend to withdraw when faced with possible conflict. "Indians traditionally have regarded the good person as one who shares his money and property with others. A man's reputation was based on what he gave away, not on what he kept. Budgeting and putting away resources for a later day for oneself is improper if others are in need."[1] Indians are oriented toward the present. Thus, goals and gratifications that are accepted in the future-oriented dominant society are difficult for Indians to understand. The Indian "frame of reference is a stable social and moral system that is fixed in the universe. The shift to the highly competitive, individualistic existence of modern urban life is an adjustment that many persons have not been able to effect."[2]

The relationships that most Indians have had with non-Indians have generally been unpleasant and incompatible with rapid urban adjustment. Although the various reservations have differed somewhat in the way they have been administered, the Bureau of Indian Affairs has generally been paternalistic in its policies and many programs have been poorly planned and executed. The control of the decision-making process by government officials has resulted in communities that are dependent, hostile, and divided regarding ways to improve the situation.

State and local agency personnel as well as whites that Indians encounter in areas adjacent to reservations often have treated the latter with disdain. Therefore, the Indian may regard his new white urban neighbors and fellow workers with distrust and indifference. Thus, there is a strong tendency for migrants to limit interaction to members of his own tribe or other native Americans.

Indians must react to a variety of novel problems in the city. Reservation Indians depend on the federal government for many services that are delivered through the auspices of the Bureau of Indian Affairs and the Indian Health

Service. As indicated previously, Indians generally pay little or no rent and they receive free medical and dental care from the U.S. Public Health Service. In contrast urban dwellers must pay for these services. Money management and appropriate interaction with businessmen are skills that must be acquired.

Indians who migrate to urban areas through federal programs receive money and services from the Bureau of Indian Affairs for a limited period of time (usually one year). When they are referred to community agencies, Indians are usually not sufficiently aggressive to obtain much assistance. Often their shyness and reticence about discussing their personal problems with non-Indian strangers is regarded as a lack of cooperation. Also, the fact that appointments are scheduled at certain specific times causes difficulty for many Indians. If there is one or more Indian employees working in a community agency native Americans generally will approach them for services. Indian centers and those private agencies that have tried to develop a special understanding of their Indian clients such as the American Friends Service Committee have been the chief organizations contacted by Indians for welfare and personal services (see chapter 7).

The poverty of underdeveloped reservations has brought about a continuing migration of American Indians to urban areas. A clear understanding by urban community agencies of the unique cultural characteristics of their Indian clients and of how these characteristics affect their adaptation and adjustment is a necessary prelude to working effectively with recently migrated Indians.

Indians do not possess any of the common attributes generally associated with distinctive ethnic and minority groups. Racial distinctiveness is not usually an attribute that is applied to Indians in the ethnological or anthropological sense. Indians may possess racial characteristics that are very similar to those of Caucasians while others have racial characteristics that are more "Oriental." North American Indians have sometimes been designated as "members of the red race."[3] Racial categorization is not universally accepted as there is so much diversity in the physical characteristics of these people. However, they are all labeled "Indian" and their subsequent treatment is influenced by this identification.

Table 8-1 indicates some of the factors that serve to differentiate the process of urban Indian assimilation and adjustment from those of other immigrant and migrant groups.

Urban Indian *acculturation* involves replacing or modifying his reservation culture, as well as acquiring new behavioral traits. Indices of acculturation include type of recreational activities, formal education, occupation and the loss of ability to use an Indian language.

Adjustment—as a dimension of psychological and social health—can be measured by such factors as suicide rates, confinement in mental hospitals, crime rates, and jobless rates.

Adjustment and acculturation are not always positively correlated. For example, military service seems to have a negative effect on Indian adjustment to white culture but a positive effect on acculturation to white society.

Table 8-1
Characteristics of Migrant Groups to Urban Areas

Acknowledged Characteristics	Rural Migrant	Foreign Immigrant	Indian Migrant
Common ethnicity	No	Yes	No
Proximity to home	Yes	No	Sometimes Yes
Common culture	No	No	No
Strong family ties	No	Yes	Usually Yes
"Ghetto" urban formation	No	Yes	Sometimes Yes
Language problems	No	Yes	Yes
Cultural traits			
1. Saving and security	Yes	Yes	No
2. Established organization	Yes	Yes	No
3. Common language	Yes	Yes	No

Source: Adapted from Mark Nagler, *Indians in the City: A Study of the Urbanization of Indians in Toronto* (Ottawa, Canada: St. Paul University, 1973), p. 67.

Martin found in Dallas that the Navajo were relatively well adjusted to urban life. The kind of passive adjustment which occurred can take place with minimal acculturation. According to Kluckohn and Leighton, "Navajos are distinguished among American Indians by the alacrity if not the ease with which they have adjusted to the impact of white culture while still retaining many native traits and preserving the framework of their own cultural organization."[4] Martin indicates that Navajo men are less adjusted than Navajo women, while Price shows Navajo men to be more acculturated than the women.

Models of Acculturation and Adjustment

Martin studied the adjustment of Navajos, Sioux, and Choctaws in Dallas. He used the following criteria to classify behavioral adjustment[5]

1. Good: Evidence indicates no serious problems; seems highly motivated; may become successful and then return to the reservation.
2. Satisfactory: Evidence of problems but shows signs of adjustment—holds job, gets jobs on his own, cooperative; may start poorly but improves.
3. Fair: Evidence of problems and attempts to overcome them without too much success—continues to have difficulties in spite of personal effort; may start well but performance declines.
4. Poor: Evidence of poor job performance—absenteeism, quitting jobs, excessive drinking, or arrests.
5. Poor: Evidence of poor motivation (other than in 4)—lack of cooperation

128

with BIA personnel, fails to keep appointments, refuses certain jobs, complains about hard work or the weather.

Adaptive-like behavior (high adjustment rating) is displayed more frequently by the Navajo, followed in order by the Choctaw and Sioux. In general, younger men tend to show better behavioral adjustment than older men, particularly among the Navajo. Military experience and an arrest record prior to relocation appears to have a negative influence on adjustment. The negative influence of military experience is greatest among those persons remaining in the military less than two years.[6]

The relatively better showing of the Navajo is not readily explained on the basis of acculturation unless one is willing to argue a low quantity-high quality acculturation thesis. As indicated previously, it is possible that the passive and cooperative native of the Navajo is the most plausible explanation for their better performance and adjustment.[7] If this is correct, important questions occur. Does the Navajo really adapt better or does he simply give less trouble? Are there characteristics that assist adaptation during the early stages of an urban migration but which prove maladaptive over the long run?

According to Broom and Kitsuse, many American Indians are attempting to "validate their acculturation by moving into the larger stream of life."[8] Many of them are not sufficiently acculturated to function well within non-Indian society. However, the acculturative experience of some has been sufficiently negative to have had a corrosive effect on their behavior. Since Indian communities and parallel ethnic institutions are in an immature stage of development in some cities,[9] relocated Indians sometimes lack the supportive functions a more mature structure could provide. It is unclear whether Pan-Indian enclave communities will develop in these cities or whether Indians will bypass this stage and be directly assimilated into urban society.[a]

Hurt studied the urbanizing Sioux of Yankton, South Dakota—a small city with a population of nearly 10,000. He classified Indians into three types: the rejecting Indians, the selecting Indians, and the accepting Indians.[10]

The urban rejecting Indian reacts negatively to his environment. Their behavior results in frequent contact with the law regarding charges of vagrancy, public intoxication, and disturbing the peace. Thus, when not wandering they spent much time in jail. They are not oriented to Indian culture, nor do they identify with the dominant value system. In larger cities these Indians are usually found on skid row.

Selecting Indians display a varied behavior and ideology while having some important characteristics in common. They do not completely accept either the cultural pattern of the reservation or the dominant tradition of the city of Yankton. These Indians can be subdivided into two major classifications:

[a]As indicated in chapter 5, Indian population concentrations presently exist in a number of cities. However, in no sense are these Pan-Indian ethnic communities.

(1) The reservation-oriented Indian who in turn can be categorized into two subtypes—

(a) The seasonal migratory laborers who come to Yankton to find summer employment at the box factory, seed company, and in outdoor construction projects. At the end of the summer, when work is completed, they return to the reservation. For these Indians the preservation of Indian values is of major importance.

(b) The permanent or long-time residents are characterized by a great desire to return to the reservation and by an intense dislike of the city. The primary reason for moving to Yankton is economic improvement. If these Indians could make an adequate living on the reservation they would return. Retention of Indian identity is important to them and they would like to have their children be able to speak the Dakota Sioux language.

and (2) the urban-oriented residents—These Indians also have a critical attitude toward living in Yankton but have even less desire to live on a reservation. Although claiming to have left the reservation primarily for economic betterment, they indicate that they would not return there even if jobs were available. In Yankton the urban-oriented Indian usually finds difficulty in adjusting to the community as a whole. Thus, they tend to associate with other Indians and low-income whites.[11]

The accepting Indian is both highly critical and ashamed of Indians and Indian culture. Reservations are seldom visited and when they are, it is only for business or to see a very close friend or relative.

The proportion of Indians which can be placed in each of the categories described is indicated in table 8-2.

Following Gordon's conceptualization,[12] Chadwick and Strauss use a seven-stage model of assimilation in their study of American Indians in Seattle.[13]

Table 8-2
Proportion of Indians with Various Types of Urban Adjustment

Classification	Percentage
1. Rejecting	1
2. Selecting	80
A. Reservation-oriented	
1) Season at migratory	20
2) Permanent or long-time residents	20
B. Urban oriented	40
3. Accepting	19

Source: Adapted from Wesley Hurt, Jr., "The Urbanization of the Yankton Indians," *Human Organization* (Winter, 1961-1962): 228-230.

Cultural or behavioral assimilation was measured by three attitude scales supportive of Indians blending into American society as well as self-reported behavior indicating such involvement. The self-reported activities were educational attainment, employment, occupational status, income, religious preference, ability to speak a native language, and attendance at powwows.

Marital assimilation was indicated by marriage to a white, having family members married to a white, and degree of Indian ancestry.

Identificational assimilation was measured by the person's feelings regarding how he or she fit into white society and their self-identification as being Indian or white.

Attitude receptional assimilation was indicated by having negative stereotypes concerning Indians and a rejection of future social interaction with Indians.

Behavior receptional assimilation was assessed by individually reported discrimination experienced by Indians in the two years preceding the study and by perceptions of discrimination by both whites and Indians.

Civic assimilation was determined by three attitude scales and self-reported protest activity concerning the turning over of surplus federal lands to Indians and fishing rights.

Structural assimilation was determined by the amount of time one has lived in an urban area (as a percentage of their total life experience), the number of organizational memberships, the extent of regular social interaction with members of other races, and a structural assimilation scale combining home ownership, current employment, and marital status.

The results obtained by Chadwick and Strauss indicate that Indians living in Seattle are not assimilated to any significant degree into the dominant society.[14] Regular attendance at powwows and the retention of a native language reveal an intent by Indians to preserve at least a part of the Indian way of life. This dual lifestyle—combining participation in white society while retaining Indian ways— is also apparent in strong Indian self-identity. Although cultural pluralism seems a responsible compromise (consistent with a feeling of respect for cultural differences), the overall effect is that urban Indian assimilation has been retarded.

Assimilation, Acculturation and Adjustment—Some Case Studies

Although numerous articles have described the level of assimilation, acculturation, or amalgamation of various tribes, particularly those residing on reservations, there is a paucity of information concerning assimilation of native Americans living in cities. The standard assumption is that migration to the city results in greater assimilation.

There is little evidence that assimilation has, in fact, occurred and currently some Indian organizations are arguing that Indians in cities are not integrated into society but are an alienated, invisible minority group. Such organizations are insisting that the BIA recognize the unique problems confronted by urban Indians and sponsor programs designed to assist them to improve their economic and social status in the city.

Although many Oneida leave the home community, there are still various social and emotional links between those on the reservation and those who leave. There is a considerable amount of two-way visiting by members of both groups. Many of those who live in Milwaukee and Chicago return to their homeland for weekends, powwows, and holidays. Others come back to be married in Oneida churches and later return to have their children baptized or christened there. In addition, many who left Oneida when they were in the prime working ages return to the Oneida community to retire, a pattern which has important economic consequences for the community.[15] Finally, at the time of death, the bodies of many emigrants are returned for burial in local cemeteries.

Oneidas believe that the major obstacle to employment in Green Bay (the nearest off-reservation city) is the widespread anti-Indian prejudice of that city's employers. The Oneida say that they do not experience such prejudice in Milwaukee, Chicago, Detroit, and other cities located a considerable distance from the reservation. Consequently, they continue to leave the community despite a preference for living in Oneida.[16]

Most Oneida can relate anecdotal cases of prejudice that either they or their relatives have experienced. Such anecdotal, nonstatistical data cannot prove that extensive prejudice exists in Green Bay. However, the fact that the Oneida *believe* that such prejudice exists, explains part of the continuing outmigration of workers.

Price surveyed migrants to Los Angeles regarding life on the reservation, life in the city, and the factors which led individuals to migrate.[17] The pattern of responses was similar to that which might be expected from Euro-Americans who had migrated to a large city from a rural or small town background. The incentive for migration was primarily economic, that is to find jobs, to obtain higher wages, and to improve their living conditions. Los Angeles Indians tend to dislike the smog, urban crowding, transportation problems, and high cost of living in the city; and they fondly remember the social contacts and activities they had on the reservation. Over time they increasingly withdraw from previous reservation contacts (fewer returns to the reservation, fewer letters), while concomitantly they increasingly tend to idealize the physical and cultural aspects of reservation life. Many older urban Indians wish to retire to their home reservations, particularly if they own property there.

Price's findings tend to validate the assertion of Nancy Lurie that "the option to assimilate is far more open for Indians than for almost any other minority."[18] The movement from a reservation where the vast majority of the population is Indian, to a city where native Americans are a tiny minority, is a major step toward assimilation into white society. However, the Indian also has the option to continue relating to other urban Indians. Los Angeles contains a variety of Indian social groups (kinship, tribal Pan-Indian clubs or centers) with which Indians affiliate in varying degrees.

Indians generally (and especially the Sioux) tend to accept the responsibility of helping their relatives or tribesmen when asked, and will readily give money, food, or lodging to a needy family. The flexibility of the Indian household is often vast, and most Indian families are willing to make room for five or six additional persons at meals or for lodging, even if they have only limited food or space for themselves. However, some families leave town or keep their place of residence secret because they have been overwhelmed with requests for assistance, which they did not feel they could refuse.[19]

Most Indian relocatees living in the San Francisco area indicated to Ablon that they would return home to their reservations immediately if they could find employment there. The lack of job opportunities and the variety of social problems characteristic of most reservations preclude the likelihood that many who have found steady work will return home, except for brief periods of time.

Navajos in San Francisco frequently tend to associate almost exclusively with other Navajos. They interact with persons of their own age group who are either relatives or those they have met in their neighborhood or at formal group occasions. Navajos tend to be more restricted socially than persons from other tribes chiefly because of their very traditional tribal background, their shyness and reticence (particularly in the presence of non-Navajos), and a strong fear of English language inadequacy. Many Navajos began school at a relatively late age and obtained only an elementary school education. Even those who frequently were employed outside the reservation prefer to limit their association to fellow Navajos and speak to whites as little as possible. Their sensitivity about their halting speech often results in a strong anxiety about dealing with non-Navajo speakers. Most of the Navajos in the San Francisco Bay area appear to have only limited interest in any kind of formal activity, whether Navajo, Pan-Indian, or white in origin.[20]

Although many Indians responded that they had white friends as well as Indians, Ablon determined that most relationships established with whites were relatively superficial ones, consisting of those with fellow workers with whom they ate lunch, and with white neighbors with whom they sometimes conversed or had a cup of coffee. Usually such relationships with whites could be classified more accurately as acquaintances than friendships.

Some Indians who come to the city often exhibit a neo-Indian social identity which is Pan-Indian in its origin. Thus, alumni of Haskell Institute exhibit a Pan-Indian social focus by associating more readily with persons of other tribes than do most other Indians.[b] The fact that they attended Haskell Institute often is of more importance to them than common tribal identity. In general, these neo-Indians are often highly educated and well dressed. Many have the social skills and comparable material possessions to allow them to enter white society if they wished, but they consistently choose to associate almost exclusively with Indians. As Ablon describes it, "a positive continuing sense of personal and social identity is the chief factor in the social segregation of Indians. The fact of Indian identity seems to determine the choice of looking to Indian groups to find one's friends."[21]

Theodore Graves has related personality traits of Navajos in Denver to factors indicating economic success and personal adjustment.[22] The personality traits considered are an extended future time perspective, feelings of personal control over one's destiny, and achievement motivation. Surprisingly the variables were not directly related to economic performance or maladjustment as measured by the incidence of heavy drinking or arrests.

Those migrants receiving low wages in the city and who have strong feelings of fatalism appear to be resigned to continuing failure, and their arrest rates are much higher than those with similar economic experiences who believe they are capable of influencing the future. An extended future time perspective and a strong achievement motivation have a strong relationship to arrest rates among those with economic problems, but in the opposite direction of Graves' expectations. Those with more extended time perspective have higher arrest rates if they are doing poorly in the city, perhaps because they expect their present lack of success to continue in the future or because they suffer from greater anxiety than those who live for the present. Moreover, those with high achievement motivation feel more acutely the effect of economic failure than those less strongly committed to succeed. Thus, those with extended time perspective and high achievement motivation are more likely to get drunk.[23]

The applied implications of these findings are clear. Rather than allocating resources in a useless effort to foster a middle-class personality among Indians, the Bureau of Indian Affairs and its counselors and teachers should increase the effort to provide native Americans with marketable skills. Moreover, non-Indian employers must make more jobs available to Indians. As Parker and Kleiner point out, "a middle-class personality is adaptive only within a structural setting which permits the attainment of middle-class goals. Otherwise, such psychological traits tend to be maladaptive and to create additional adjustment problems for those who have acquired them. Interestingly, identical empirical findings are available for urban blacks."[24]

---

[b]Haskell Institute in Lawrence, Kansas generally is considered to have been the best Indian boarding school in the country. Haskell offered academic and vocational high school curriculums and postgraduate vocational training. Many Haskell graduates took jobs in the San Francisco area each year. More recently Haskell Institute has been converted to a junior college.

Finally, if these middle-class personality traits are not directly linked to higher income, and if the absence of the former is not a source of adjustment problems when wages are relatively good, a reassessment of the importance of these traits is in order. There is increasing evidence that the anthropological concept of cultural (and psychological) relativism is highly significant in this context. Thus, it appears that minority group critics of educational programs aimed at changing their lifestyle, rather than that of the dominant society, have some empirical justification for their position.[25]

The urban adjustment of Kiowa Indians to the San Francisco Bay area can be described as an example of the process of compartmentalization. Through employment, the migrant Kiowa participates in the economic affairs of the city but never really commits himself to the economic aspirations of his fellow non-Indian employees. He appreciates the income from steady wage work, but never separates himself from the Oklahoma Kiowa. He utilizes the economic advantages of the city to strengthen his tribal image in both the city and in his home community.[26]

Away from his place of employment, the Kiowa is totally oriented to his own community. He recognizes his obligations to both urban and rural relatives, and spends much of his time representing the Kiowa viewpoint in the San Francisco area Pan-Indian movement. He has limited social contacts with non-Indians and their institutions. His primary activities occur among other native Americans. The Kiowa is a part-time Indian in his relationship to the dominant society. He utilizes this society as a reference group to determine his role in the non-Indian culture.

The migrant Kiowa uses two reference groups in the process of compart-mentalizing his roles in the urban area. The white society is used as described and the rural Kiowa society serves as the second reference group or anchor culture.

Thus, the migrant Kiowa is able to maintain his tribal identity within the urban setting. He utilizes his relationships with the dominant urban society to obtain the economic benefits of the city. Part of his income is used in family maintenance, housing, food, transportation, and other necessities. The remainder is employed to maintain the Kiowa system of obligations to urban and rural relatives.

The Kiowa views his job as an activity requiring a commitment of eight hours of hard work. He does not concern himself with job-related problems while at home nor does he aspire for job advancement. The Kiowa seldom look for another position once they have obtained steady employment and relatively good wages. They rarely participate in labor disputes since they believe that their employment is based on a personal contract between the worker and his immediate supervisor. He does associate with his fellow employees if they are Indian, but most contact with non-Indians at home and at work is avoided.[27]

The Kiowa case presents an example of urban adjustment differing in several respects from other tribes that have relocated to San Francisco. The Kiowa have not formed an ethnic enclave as the Navajo have done. The Navajo have been able to transplant virtually their entire reservation culture to San Francisco. As indicated, they keep to themselves, live in very close proximity to one another, speak the Navajo language, and function as much as possible like Navajos on the reservation. The Navajo rarely participate in Pan-Indian movements. They are more concerned about retaining the Navajo community and its traditional practices.

The Sioux in San Francisco are also concerned about the maintenance of traditional Sioux culture. They have little problem establishing identity since this tribe has always been well known by non-Sioux Indians. The Sioux have tended to maintain group solidarity by carrying out traditional functions. The Sioux have also tended to isolate themselves and rarely participate in Pan-Indian organizations.

In contrast to the Sioux and Navajo, the Kiowa make full use of outsiders to further their cause in urban society. The economic system of the dominant culture is employed by the migrant Kiowa to provide money for survival in the city, as well as to provide assistance to relatives. The latter reinforces the Kiowa kinship system and allows greater participation in the development of an urban Indian culture.[28]

Some Policy Implications

There seems to be some growth in Pan-Indian feelings or in tribal communities that is resulting in the creation of institutional means of preserving Indian ways. This may seriously retard the assimilation process. The emphasis on Indian culture in various heritage programs, which includes values and behavioral patterns that are incompatible with an urban industrial society, may also hinder, if not reverse, the assimilation process. However, some Indians contend that it is too psychologically punishing to have to relate nearly simultaneously to Indian and white values and behaviors.

An additional factor contributing to the lack of assimilation of Indians into urban society is the amount of active economic and social discrimination practiced against Indians. Hostility and prejudice limit many educational and occupational opportunities for native Americans and prevent the informal interaction which would certainly accelerate assimilation.

Policy makers, program administrators, and individual Indians must recognize that one major effect of relocation is to shift Indian problems into the city where they are less visible. The assimilation versus pluralism question needs to be carefully considered. If assimilation is one of the major goals of relocation, then programs can be developed to make assimilation as painless as possible. One very important policy implication would be to reverse the practice of denying urban

Indians the health and social service programs which are available to reservation Indians. Some progress is being made through the courts in extending these services. In February 1974, the U.S. Supreme Court ordered the Bureau of Indian Affairs to provide service to a Papago Indian who had left the reservation to work in the mines at Ajo, Arizona.[29] This ruling was not a sweeping decision since it specified certain conditions necessary for Indians living off the reservation to receive BIA services, but it does represent a significant step forward. Increasing the BIA's sensitivity to the needs of urban Indians would certainly help their adjustment to urban living. In addition, programs to provide training and assistance in coping with urban institutions such as the police and courts, merchants, banks, landlords, and government agencies, would greatly facilitate Indian participation in urban society.

Perhaps one solution to the dilemma between assimilation and pluralism could be to permit the individual migrant to choose between the two possibilities. Thus, those who desire to assimilate would be given assistance to become a functioning member of the urban community while those who did not wish it could live in the city and still maintain some of their Indian heritage.

Summary

The uniqueness of reservation culture has made native American adjustment to urban society difficult and psychologically painful. Some traditional Indian values are simply incompatable with those of the dominant culture.

Three models of acculturation and adjustment were discussed. In each situation considerable resistance to assimilation by native Americans was found with most Indians limiting the social interactions to members of their own tribe or native Americans of other tribes.

Among Indian migrants to San Francisco, the Kiowa are most active in the support and development of a Pan-Indian movement while simultaneously maintaining the traditional culture of the Oklahoma Kiowa. The Navajo and Sioux, in contrast, limit their contacts to their fellow tribesmen as much as possible and do not support Pan-Indian movements.

One policy which would encourage assimilation would be the federal provision of some of the services to urban Indians that the BIA makes available to reservation Indians. If these services were provided the migrant would have a meaningful choice between assimilation and some degree of cultural separatism.

Notes

1. Joan Ablon, "Cultural Conflict in Urban Indians," *Mental Hygiene* 55, no. 2 (April 1971): 203.

2. Ibid.

3. Mark Nagler, *Indians in the City: A Study of the Urbanization of Indians in Toronto* (Ottawa, Canada: St. Paul University, 1973), p. 67.

4. Clyde Klucksohn and Dorothea Leighton, *The Navajo* (New York: Doubleday, 1962), p. 17.

5. Harry Martin, "Correlates of Adjustment Among American Indians in an Urban Environment," *Human Organization* 23, no. 4 (Winter 1964): 295.

6. Ibid., p. 294.

7. Dorothea Leighton and Clyde Klucksohn, *Children of the People* (Cambridge, Massachusetts: Harvard University Press, 1947), p. 107.

8. Leonard Broom and John Kitsuse, "The Validation of Acculturation: A Condition to Assimilation," *American Anthropologist* 47 (February 1955): 44-45.

9. Ibid. That is institutions within ethnic communities having the essential characteristics of institutional forms of the larger society.

10. Wesley Hurt, "The Urbanization of the Yankton Indians," *Human Organization* (Winter 1962): 226-231.

11. Ibid., p. 229.

12. M.M. Gordon, *Assimilation in American Life: The Role of Race, Religion, and Natural Origins* (New York: Oxford University Press, 1964).

13. Bruce A. Chadwick and Joseph H. Strauss, "The Assimilation of American Indians into Urban Society," *Human Organization* 34, no. 4 (Winter 1975): 363.

14. Ibid., p. 366.

15. John Dowling, "A 'Rural' Indian Community in an Urban Setting," *Human Organization* 27, no. 3 (Fall 1968): 238.

16. Ibid., p. 239.

17. John A. Price, "The Migration and Adaptation of American Indians to Los Angeles," *Human Organization* 27, no. 2 (Summer 1968): 171.

18. Nancy O. Lurie, "The Enduring Indian," *Natural History* 75, no. 9 (1966): 10-22.

19. Joan Ablon, "Relocated American Indians in the San Francisco Bay Area: Social Interaction and Indian Identity," *Human Organization* 23, no. 4 (1964): 298.

20. Ibid., p. 299.

21. Ibid., p. 303.

22. Theodore Graves, "Urban Indian Personality and the Culture of Poverty," *American Ethnologist* (1974): 65-86.

23. Ibid., p. 83.

24. Seymour Parker and Robert Kleiner, "The Culture of Poverty: An Adjustive Dimension," *American Anthropologist* 72 (1970): 516-527.

25. Graves, "Urban Indian Personality," p. 83.

26. Gordon Krutz, "Compartmentalization as a Factor in Urban Adjust-

ment: The Kiowa Case," in Jack O. Waddell and O. Michael Watson, eds., *American Indian Urbanization* (Lafayette, Indiana: Purdue University, Institute for the Study of Social Change, 1973), Institute Monograph Series No. 4, pp. 101-102.

27. Ibid., p. 105.

28. Ibid., p. 111.

29. Chadwick and Strauss, "The Assimilation of American Indians," p. 368.

Summary, Conclusions, and Recommendations

There is little doubt that the social and economic problems presently confronting many urban Indians are nearly overwhelming. In many cities unemployment rates are very high. The average income of urban Indians lags far behind that of most city dwellers. An unduly high number of Indians are forced to subsist solely on welfare payments, private charity, or handouts from relatives. There is a housing crisis, far too many migrant Indians are living in the slums of our metropolitan areas. They are forced to struggle daily with the problems of vice and crime which are rampant in our inner cities. Native Americans face nearly overwhelming problems coping with the city school system. Dropout rates are very high (even greater than on the reservations), and achievement levels are generally low. Indians complain of prejudice and discrimination in the schools and an irrelevant curriculum. The average health status of urban Indians is poor, perhaps even worse than is the case among their reservation counterparts. Lack of access to urban health services and dental care force many Indians to return to the home reservation for care. Alcoholism is a major problem. Many newly arrived migrants gravitate to skid row and an existence centered around the bottle and the bar. Unfortunately the bar is often the only place where Indians can go to meet their friends or fellow tribesmen.

Indian centers and other Indian organizations, such as clinics, alcoholism treatment programs, and church-related agencies, have struggled against heavy odds to improve the quality of life for the urban Indian. However, factionalism, staff turnover, and the competition for the limited funds available have impaired the effectiveness of these organizations.

Before proceeding with detailed recommendations for improvement, it is necessary to indicate three major assumptions being made regarding appropriate urban federal policy. These assumptions underlie all subsequent discussion.

1. That an appropriate interpretation of the Snyder Act of 1921 requires that the federal government provide services to urban Indians consistent with demonstrated need. Since this has not been the existing policy, specific enabling legislation may have to be passed by Congress in order for this to occur (see chapter 1).

The major argument against such a change in policy is that Indians in cities should be treated like any other urban poor population—no special programs are needed. Thus, social service agencies should attempt to meet the needs of their Indian clients as they would any other person in need of assistance.

Such a position ignores not only the unique culture of the American Indian, but does not consider the fact that over 150,000 Indians have been relocated at government expense from the reservation to the city. For the government to induce a movement of this magnitude and provide only minimal services thereafter is cruel. Moreover, as there is no administratively feasible way of limiting assistance to only urban Indians relocated under federal auspices, help should be given to all urban Indians who need it—and most do.

2. That one single agency be established to administer all Indian programs both for reservation and urban Indians. Such an agency would permit the coordination of various programs more effectively if total responsibility were placed in one department. Moreover, such an organization would provide the Indians better access to the program and funding personnel with whom they must deal concerning new or existing programs.

At present there are nine cabinet-level departments and ten individual agencies that operate programs for American Indians. Many of these programs duplicate each other. For example, the Bureau of Indian Affairs and the Department of Labor offer manpower programs with overlapping objectives. Business and commercial development is the responsibility of the Economic Development Administration, the Office of Minority Business Enterprise, and the Small Business Administration. Agricultural development is the concern of the Bureau of Indian Affairs, Branch of Land Operations, and the Department of Agriculture.

Moreover, the consolidation of all Indian programs into one agency would permit a much greater degree of emphasis to be placed on monitoring and evaluation than has occurred previously. In the past different definitions of who is a native American as well as varying methods of evaluation, have made it nearly impossible to determine which agencies were doing a good job on behalf of native Americans and which were not.

3. That a crash effort be made to establish a reliable set of statistics regarding the social and economic conditions and program needs of urban Indians. Many studies have been critical of the federal government because of the paucity of such information in regard to reservation Indians. However, the situation is far worse for urban Indians where even such basic information as the Indian population in various cities is not really known. Such studies could be undertaken by the Bureau of the Census in conjunction with a number of representative Indian organizations. Without the participation of the latter, individual cooperation will be difficult to attain.

Health

The health problems of Indians living in urban areas have not been well documented. The information available implies considerably higher rates of mortality and morbidity from infectious diseases than for non-Indian urban dwellers. The difficulties of adjusting to life in a city have created significant problems in terms of Indian mental health. Finally, alcoholism is probably the most important health problem among urban Indians. Present methods of treatment have made a minimal impact on the incidence of this disease.

The first recommendation is to create a network of federally funded urban Indian health centers. Such centers would offer comprehensive medical and dental care to all Indians with charges related to income. Low-income Indians would receive care free of charge, but others would be expected to pay for care. The health center should be located in the area where the Indian population is concentrated, with satellite clinics developed to serve other areas with fewer numbers of Indians.

These clinics should not only offer curative medical services, but should include a major preventive component as well. Preventive services in the areas of prenatal care, nutrition, and drug and alcohol abuse are vitally needed.

In addition, psychiatric and other mental health services should be provided. As discussed in chapter 8, many Indians find the adjustment from the quiet, slow-paced reservation life to the noisy competitive pace of the city a difficult one. A good mental health service staffed by Indians who are familiar with the problem of urban acculturation and adjustment could make the difference between making a successful adaptation to the city life or becoming a member of the bar crowd and ending up on skid row.

Alcoholism treatment programs should be funded *through the clinics* not only because alcoholics have other health problems, but because alcoholism is a disease. Moreover, persons with alcohol problems often need mental health services, and it would be most convenient if all of these services were provided by one organization.

To develop service packages that address most effectively the total health needs of the urban Indian, an urban Indian health information system needs to be established. This would permit the determination of the relative severity of particular diseases or conditions among Indians as well as the effectiveness over time of the centers themselves in improving the health status of the urban Indian.

Research into the causes of and most effective means of treating urban Indian alcoholism is critically necessary. There are many competing hypotheses in the literature, but Graves' work represents the only solid empirical study in the field. It is possible that controlled studies testing different methods of treatment could be undertaken.

There is a great need for trained alcoholism counselors and other professionals in this field who are native Americans. Training programs must be expanded well beyond the present $1 million in funding so that Indian alcoholics can receive therapy from a trained native.

Finally, as indicated in chapter 4, many urban Indians still utilize traditional Indian medicine. Some research is necessary to determine which of the practices are harmful to health status, which are neutral, and which have positive effects. A health education program aimed at reducing the use of harmful practices would then be appropriate.

It is recommended that $75 million be made available for development and expansion of urban Indian health centers. This is a major increase when compared to the $3 million presently spent on urban Indian health and $5 million allocated to alcoholism; but $75 million is less than 15 percent of the amount spent on these activities for programs which serve reservation Indians.

Manpower Programs

According to the standard criteria used to evaluate manpower programs the relocation and AVT programs operated by the Bureau of Indian Affairs have been quite successful (see chapter 3). However, there is evidence that in recent years a decline in admission standards has resulted in fewer trainees being placed in jobs as well as a higher percentage of relocatees returning home after a short period of time in the city.

Opportunities should continue to be made available for reservation Indians to come to urban areas for employment and training. Given the high rate of unemployment on the reservations (40 percent), off-reservation employment opportunities are the only way that many native Americans will ever have the opportunity to obtain steady work. However, the program must remain completely *voluntary*.

There is no evidence that the CETA program, with its emphasis on institutional and on-the-job training, has been any more successful in training and placing graduates than has the Bureau of Indian Affairs.

The consolidation of manpower programs operated by the Bureau of Indian Affairs and the Department of Labor into one program should eliminate duplication of effort and reduce administrative costs.

One major problem in training and placing graduates is that little information exists regarding the number of jobs available in specific labor markets. A detailed study is needed concerning job availability in various metropolitan areas for persons with the kinds of skills trainees will obtain. Once this information is available, training programs can channel workers into the occupations with the greatest relative shortage and thus reduce urban Indian unemployment. Given the present level of unemployment among urban Indians and the expected continued flow of Indians from the reservations to the city—with or without government assistance—the level of expenditures for urban manpower programs should be greatly increased.

Increases in expenditures from $40 million to $100 million should allow all those who want training to obtain it. This level of funding should also allow an increase in the subsistence allowances paid to trainees so that they do not have to undergo privation while they are enrolled in training programs.

Research is badly needed to determine which age, sex, and tribal groups are most likely to benefit from training. For example, surveys made by the BIA in the mid 1960s indicated that single women soon left the labor force after training had been completed. If this situation still prevails, a reasonable policy would be to minimize the number of single women admitted to the training programs.

The procedures for evaluating manpower programs are well known. A rigorous and continued program of evaluation should permit the development of a comprehensive effort that is capable of significantly reducing both urban and rural Indian unemployment and raising individual incomes substantially.

As the urban Indian population has grown, many day labor contractors have begun operating store-front offices in Indian neighborhoods. Such organizations should be closely regulated by state and local agencies to reduce the possibility of exploitation of the Indian worker by the daily-pay organization. Moreover, Indian organizations should consider following the example of Minneapolis and moving actively into the field of day-labor contracting to prevent non-Indian dominance in this sphere. However, this should be a short-run strategy; in the long run, Indian organizations should orient Indian workers toward better paying *permanent* jobs.

Anecdotal information indicates widespread employment discrimination against Indian workers by non-Indian employers. Federal, state, and local civil rights laws must be rigorously enforced and Indian individuals and organizations must file suit when it is likely that discrimination has occurred.

Federal grants should be given to universities and other appropriate organizations to undertake research regarding the magnitude and dimensions of anti-Indian discrimination. Such research could determine what types of discrimination are most prevalent (employment, housing, police, and courts), and whether there are variations in the intensity of anti-Indian discrimination by region or reservation-urban residence.

Indian Centers and Related Organizations

Indian centers have developed (primarily during the 1960s) in most urban areas with large Indian populations. They have been most useful in offering emergency services, referrals for services to non-Indian agencies, as well as providing the impetus for the development of social and athletic events within the Indian community.

Core funding has been forthcoming from the Office of Native American Programs under legislation passed in 1974. Financial resources are provided on a per capita basis but no grant can exceed $200,000. Since population estimates for urban Indians are very inaccurate this is an inappropriate method for funding. The size of grants should be based on demonstrated need for services as well as the capacity of the organization to effectively deliver a service package.

Some Indian organizations have tried to develop competence in too many different activities simultaneously and have offered an uneven bundle of services.

One of the most pressing problems is the competition between Indian organizations for the limited funding available. Priority should be given to proposals in which several organizations agree to work together in the provision of services. The problems of factionalism and tribal differences do not seem solvable in the short run. One would expect that over time, the intensity of these feelings should diminish and the appropriate steps could be taken toward the development of a true Pan-Indian movement.

Although precise service needs cannot be established at this time because of lack of information, Indian centers and related organizations have not been able to reach more than a fraction of those requiring assistance. This is particularly the case among older Indians, whose lack of transportation and limited schooling signal a need for special assistance. Initially the level of appropriation for Indian service organizations should be increased from $5 million to $15 million.

Housing and Social Services

Urban Indian housing conditions are deplorable. Most families are renters living in decaying apartments in slum areas. Rents take up a large share of income. Prejudice and discrimination keep Indians out of more desirable neighborhoods. Indians are reluctant to move into public housing projects because of the high proportion of tenants in many cities who are black. Indians generally do not wish to live or associate with blacks.

The Department of Housing and Urban Development and the Bureau of Indian Affairs provide six different housing programs for reservation Indians. A home purchase program for Indians relocated to urban areas under the auspices of the BIA was dropped in the early 1970s. Urban Indians receive no specific housing services from the federal government at the present time, but are eligible to apply for programs available to the general population.

The federal government should provide several major programs to urban Indians that have been available to reservation Indians since the 1960s. The first is low-rent housing which operates on reservations much as it does in other parts of the nation. Indian groups in urban areas could establish housing authorities, paying for the construction with funds from the Housing Assistance Administration of the U.S. Department of Housing and Urban Development. The Indian group would determine the rents which would presumably be based on income and family size. Salaries of project employees and maintenance costs would have to be covered by rents.

The Bureau of Indian Affairs operates a Home Improvement Program with an annual budget of $11 million in 1976.[1] The program has actively operated on several northern reservations where unemployment rates are very high and a great many Indians live in dilapidated or makeshift housing. This program should be established within urban areas. It could be useful in stemming urban blight in those areas where Indian families have bought their first home. These homes are frequently run-down and need major repairs. This program could provide assistance in funding the necessary renovations.

A fairly recent approach to public housing is the turnkey method, which has been used in construction throughout the country. It allows private developers great latitude in project formulation and development. The developer supplies the site and builds the development, which is then sold to the housing authority. The procedure is quite different from the usual public housing construction process in which the housing authority acts more or less as its own general contractor. Evidence indicated that turnkey units could be built for about $3,000 less than conventional public housing units and in about one-third less time.[2] Under a variant of the turnkey program, known as Turnkey III, the local housing authority is permitted to turn the property over to the renting occupant after twenty-five years, provided the occupant has performed his own maintenance during that period. Thus, turnkey housing can be built more quickly than conventional low-rent housing, and, unlike the low-rent program, eventually it permits individual ownership.

This program which has operated on some reservations since the mid 1960s could be introduced into urban areas with an Indian organization or organizations serving as the housing authority.

Although it is difficult to estimate the total cost of an adequate urban housing program an expenditure of $20 million on the various programs discussed above would be a start toward improving housing conditions in urban Indian neighborhoods.

Indians prefer to deal with Indian-operated social service agencies. Since this often cannot be the case for social services of a general nature, these organizations should make every effort to employ Indian case workers and counselors. It may prove feasible for social service institutions to establish satellite centers in Indian neighborhoods to increase client access to services.

Most Indian children who are from broken homes are placed in non-Indian foster homes. This practice could be reduced if state and local governments would adopt more flexible standards regarding the housing and living conditions required of potential Indian foster parents. The most important aspect of the situation is to place a child in a foster home with parents that can relate well to the child. This is most likely to occur if both foster parent and child are of the same race.

Education

There is considerable ignorance concerning many aspects of urban Indian education. For example, why does the dropout rate among urban Indian youth appear to be even higher than among reservation Indian youth? It is very likely that the rate of return to secondary and postsecondary education is higher for Indians in the cities than on the reservation. Thus, human capital theory as applied to investment in education would lead one to expect urban Indians to complete school in *higher* proportions than reservation Indians. Before effective dropout prevention programs can be developed for urban Indian children, we need to know why they are dropping out. Similarly, it is known that urban Indians achieve at well below grade level in such basic skills as reading, science, and mathematics. Is the problem associated with attributes of students and their parents such as language difficulties, characteristics of the schools themselves, the teachers, the curriculum, or some or all of the above? Until acceptable answers are given to the question, "Why can't urban Indians achieve as well as non-Indians?" it makes little sense to offer detailed recommendations concerning amelioration of the problem.

To reduce the gap in educational achievement between Indians and non-Indians remedial summer school programs should be established in each city with a large Indian population. The Indian Education Act which is administered by the U.S. Office of Education could initially be the source of funding.

Alternative schools seem to be a potentially useful means of keeping some students in school who would otherwise have left. They also could be important means of increasing achievement levels. Little information is available on the strengths and weaknesses of these schools, but it does seem that the greatest need at the secondary level is for laboratory equipment and materials to teach the basic sciences—that is, biology, chemistry, and physics. If students attending these schools were able to use high quality facilities they would not be at a competitive handicap when they entered college, particularly if they wanted a scientific career or a position in one of the health fields.

The Bureau of Indian Affairs provides college scholarships to Indian students in the following order of priority: (1) reservation Indians, (2) Indians living near reservations, and (3) urban Indians. This policy should be changed so that Indians are provided college assistance on the basis of need and merit, but without regard to their place of residence.

Some Indian children who have spent much of their life on a reservation are unable to adjust to an urban school system in which the vast majority of their fellow students are non-Indian. If alternative or survival schools do not exist in that city, or are unable to accommodate all who wish to enter, then other alternatives must be sought. One alternative is to enroll these students in boarding schools operated by the Bureau of Indian Affairs primarily for reservation Indians.

The decision to undertake this action should be one in which the Indian child, his parents, and the urban school administration all agree that this transfer will be in the student's best interests. In no sense should this policy be used as a way of "dumping" problem students from cities on reservation boarding schools.

One of the greatest needs in urban Indian organizations is trained administrative personnel. An administrative training center capable of training one
hundred native administrators of Indian programs annually (both tribal and
urban) should be developed with scholarships and stipends provided in order
that administrators be freed from financial concerns while in training.

The Office of Indian Education has estimated that for the Indian Education
Act to be fully funded would require an additional $300 million or roughly
$150 million for urban Indians. This is five times the level of expenditure for
urban Indian education at the present time. While it is unrealistic to expect full
funding for this legislation given the present fiscal mood in Congress, an increase
of $150 million (evenly divided between urban and reservation Indians) would
represent a real commitment to improving the education of the first Americans.
However, an appropriation of this magnitude should not be made until the
Office of Indian Education defines its priorities carefully and develops appropriate evaluation instruments. These steps require the closest of cooperation
between the Office of Indian Education and the Indian people themselves.

Business Enterprise

Most cities have only a handful of Indian-owned businesses and the bulk of these
are very small. Expanded federal assistance is required to increase the size and
number of Indian-owned businesses. It should be expected that initially the new
enterprises will be small and that the loans and grants to a business will be of
modest size. However, over time, the average value of loans and grants awarded
will grow as businesses expand.

In addition to financial aid, expanded federal help in the form of technical
assistance and marketing research is vitally necessary. Such assistance is greatly
needed by those opening their first business enterprise.

Given the much greater assistance in business development available to
reservation as compared to urban Indians (see chapter 7), it is appropriate to
increase assistance to the latter. The sum of $20 million per year would provide
a major impetus to increasing the number of Indian-owned businesses in cities.

State and Local Assistance

Most state and local agencies of government give only minimal assistance to
reservation Indians. Since Indians pay no state or local taxes on income earned
from business activity on trust property, this position is at least partly
understandable. However, urban Indians share the same tax burdens as other
urban dwellers but often receive minimal assistance from state and local
government agencies. These organizations should not expect the federal govern-

ment to be the only public agency serving the urban Indian. All levels of government have a responsibility. One method of inducing state and local agencies to provide services to urban Indians is to tie the level of federal grants to the amount of funding the state or local government is willing to contribute. The disadvantage of such a policy is that it may penalize urban Indian groups who happen to live in a state where political leaders are not willing to make a financial commitment to the urban Indian.

Total Costs

The total increase in annual costs that would result if these recommendations were followed is summarized in table 9-1, which shows that costs would go up more than five times.

Authorization of such expenditures would not solve the problem of Indians in cities, nor are the benefits of such expenditures likely to reach all urban Indians. However, it would demonstrate the federal government's moral and legal obligation to all native Americans regardless of where they happen to reside.

Table 9-1

Annual Increase in Costs for Proposed Federal Urban Indian Programs, and 1977 Level, by Type of Program

Program	Fiscal 1977 Expenditure Reservation Indians (millions)	Fiscal 1977 Expenditure Urban Indians (millions)	Proposed Expenditure Urban Indians	Percentage Increase
Health	$420	$ 7	$ 75[a]	972
Manpower	30	10	50[b]	400
Indian centers	0	5	15	200
Housing	40	0	20	∞
Education	250[c]	30[c]	105	250
Business enterprise	10[d]	2	20	900
Total	$750	$54	$285	428

[a]Includes funding for alcoholism programs.

[b]Assumes $100 million expenditure equally divided between reservation and urban Indians.

[c]Excludes uncertain impact of U.S. Office of Education programs for general population.

[d]Excludes access to $200 million guarantee loan fund.

Notes

1. American Indian Policy Review Commission, *Final Report* (Washington, D.C.: U.S. Government Printing Office, 1977), vol. 1, p. 391.

2. Joseph Burstein, "Doors to Profit Opened Through Turnkey Program," *National News* (National Lumber and Building Material Dealers Association, April 1967).

Index

Index

Chickasaw tribe, 11
Child welfare, 80-82, 145
Child Welfare League, 82
Chippewa tribe, 11, 12
Choctaw tribe, 11, 127-128
Cirrhosis of the liver, 56
Citizenship, 2, 4
Clinton, Chadwick, and Bahr study, 32
Coleman Report, 96
College education, 20, 99, 133 n, 146
Community Action Agency Program, 113
Comprehensive Employment and Training Act (1973), 113, 114; and BIA, 39-40, 142
Creek tribe, 11
Cullum, Robert M., 34-35

Dallas: acculturation, 30, 127-128; employment and unemployment, 21, 30; health care, 52, 55; Indian institutions, 39, 108, 113
Dawes Act (1887), 2
Day labor, 40, 143
Dental care, 52
Denver: Navajo population, 30, 31, 33, 34-35, 36, 57, 58, 133
Diabetes, 50
Direct Employment Assistance Program, 25-27, 28-42 passim
Disabled, the, 78
Discrimination, 135, 143; housing, 67, 68; jobs, 30, 36-37, 40-41, 131
Disulfiram, 62
Dorothy Le Page Indian Community School (Milwaukee), 98-99
Duluth, 71

ESEA. See Elementary and Secondary Education Act
Education, 2, 87-104; achievement tests, 96, 102, 146; adult classes, 27, 95; alternative schools, 97-98, 101-102, 105 n.18, 146; attendance rates, 96-97, 101, 102; boarding schools, 90, 133, 146; Coleman Report, 96; dropout rates, 89-90,

91, 100-101, 102, 145-146; federal policy, 145-147; funding, 92-94, 98-99, 101, 102, 103, 146, 147; Indian Education Act, 95-96; science courses, 98, 146; special and remedial classes, 101, 146; state departments of, 93-94; teachers and teaching methods, 88-89, 94, 99, 101, 147. See also College education; Educational attainment; Vocational training
Education Professions Development Act, 101
Educational attainment, 18-20; as economic predictor, 31, 35, 90-91
Elderly, the, 71, 78
Elementary and Secondary Education Act (1965), 103
Employment assistance programs, 25-42, 142-143
Employment predictors, 30-31, 34-35
Episcopal Church, 117
Eskimos, 16, 58

FHA. See Federal Housing Administration
Fair Housing Act (1968), 68
Family size, as employment predictor, 35
Federal Housing Administration, 71
Field, Lemert, and Simmons study, 58
Fort Hall reservation (Idaho), 33
Foster home care, 80-82, 145
"Free schools." See Education: alternative schools

General Allotment Act (1887), 2
Graves, Theodore D., 58, 133, 141
Graves and Lave study, 30
Graves and Van Arsdale study, 35
Green Bay, Wis., 131

HEW. See United States Department of Health, Education, and Welfare
HUD. See United States Department of Housing and Urban Development
Haskell Institute, 132-133

About the Author

Alan L. Sorkin is professor and chairman of the Department of Economics at the University of Maryland Baltimore County. He also holds appointments in the Department of Preventive and Social Medicine, University of Maryland Medical School, and the Department of International Health, The Johns Hopkins School of Hygiene and Public Health. He received the Ph.D. in economics from Johns Hopkins. Dr. Sorkin is the author of *American Indians and Federal Aid* (The Brookings Institution, 1971); *Education, Unemployment, and Economic Growth* (1974), *Health Economics: An Introduction* (1975), *Health Economics in Developing Countries* (1976), and *Health Manpower: An Economic Perspective* (1977), all with Lexington Books; as well as a number of articles focusing on the economics of human resources. Lexington Books will publish his book on alternatives to the U.S. Postal Service in the near future.